SHE HEARS

Learning to Listen to Jesus

A Six-Week Bible Study By Rachael Groll

warner press®

Warner Press, Inc.
Warner Press and Warner Press logo are trademarks of Warner Press, Inc.

She Hears: Learning to Listen to Jesus

Written by Rachael Groll

Requests for information should be sent to:

Warner Press, Inc.
2902 Enterprise Drive
Anderson, IN 46013

www.warnerpress.org

Editors: Robin Loisch, Julie Campbell

Cover by Curtis Corzine

Design and Layout: Katie Miller
ISBN: 9781684343355

Printed in USA

warner press®

NOURISH the soul

TABLE OF CONTENTS

1. Mary, Mother of Jesus, *A Woman of Authority* 15

2. Samaritan Woman at the Well, *A Woman of Testimony* 41

3. Woman, *A Woman of Forgiveness* 71

4. Martha, *A Woman of Assertiveness* 97

5. Mary of Bethany, *A Woman of Discipleship* 125

6. Mary Magdalene, *A Woman of Response* 148

DEDICATION PAGE

I have had moments in my life where I have allowed my past to disqualify me from my future. That sense of failure has followed me, often to the point of pulling me back with the fear that perhaps I was not worthy of the calling I somehow found myself in. Despite my insecurities, God has placed me in a position of having influence over others. That place—that sometimes overwhelming place—is one that drives me to my knees. Through those moments, I can see and hear the Lord in a way that consumes me, to the point that I have to share it with someone—with everyone. My hope and prayer is that you would sense a little bit of what I did when I heard from the Lord, as He pressed into my heart the things He wanted me, and us, to know through this study. I am praying for you as you go, Sis. This book is dedicated to you.

Be Blessed.

Rach

INTRODUCTION

I remember very vividly the moment I came to Christ. I was a stubborn one. Jesus had been pursuing me for a while, but I, stubborn as I am, insisted that I already knew Him.

The wall was cold on my back. I leaned against it, almost as if I could push hard enough to blend in with it. I knew the questions were directed at me. I looked down, pulling at the loose threads on the sleeves of my worn Salvation Army sweatshirt. If I focused on the unraveling of the sleeves' edges, then it was easier to remain distracted from the unraveling of my heart. Everything in me wanted to scream at them. They had no idea. They could not even begin to imagine how hard it had been for me. A quick glance up revealed the differences between us, even in what we wore on our feet. Around the room were all the famous brands: Nike, Adidas, Reebok. I wore knock-off Chuck Taylors with Tweety Bird on the side from Payless. My shoes were already falling apart, but I would not be getting another pair anytime soon. The snow seeped in the seams when I walked outside, but I pretended not to notice.

"Someone in this room needs to respond to the love that He is offering." I heard the words loud and clear but pushed them away as hard as I was pushing against the wall. Not me.

Yes. You.

Nope. Not me. No way were they talking about me. I was a good kid. I got good grades. I stayed away from the stashes of drugs, alcohol, and pornography littered around my house. I kept my nose in my books. I went to bed by ten. I made sure the plants were watered and studied for tests. They were NOT talking about me.

Yes. You.

We stayed in that room a long time that night. I know they were waiting for me to respond. Instead, I focused on the strings. I still do that sometimes. I focus on something else that is unraveling, trying desperately to put it back together. It's easier than allowing myself to feel the weight of what's really going on. I wonder if you do that, too?

I kept going back, even though I knew they were disappointed in me for ignoring their pleas. Every week, the same invitation would come. And every week I would avert my eyes, close my mouth, and wait. I didn't realize at the time that I wasn't the only one waiting.

He was, too.

Eventually, because of a love that pursues us no matter how long it takes, I surrendered my heart to the One who made it. This time, I was in a room with thousands of other people, and this time, I knew exactly who the words were for.

Yes. You.

As I went forward to the altar, all I knew was that I needed the kind of love Jesus was offering. That's what drew me to Him—the love. I had been told for months that all I needed to do was receive this gift of love Jesus had for me. When I finally opened up my heart to receive what He had to offer, immediately He asked me for something more. Everything, in fact. The pain. The fear. The insecurity. The things I had been seeking and striving for. Everything.

Our response will determine our relationship.

We question and we doubt. Yet He pleads with us, "Give Me what you're holding on to."

It's not so we lose what we have. It's so we can receive what *He* has. Something so much better.

As we start to study the life of Jesus and His relationships with women found in the Book of John, my prayer is that you hear His words and realize they are not just for those women. They are for you.

Yes. You.

I don't know who you are. I don't know where you have been. I don't know what you have done. But what I do know is that we serve a God who loves you *so much* that He directed His Son, Jesus, to be here right now…in this moment…waiting for you. If you have never heard these words before or even if you have and, like me, you pushed them away, I want you to know a love that is so consuming, so intentional, and so overwhelming is being offered to you. Take a few moments and quiet your heart. Listen to what God wants to say to you.

How? How do we quiet our hearts? How do we listen? How do I *hear*?

These are questions I am asked over and over by women all over the globe.

Well, Sis, that's what we are going to discover how to do. We are going to take the next six weeks, learning to hear from the Lord.

First, we will take a look at the women in the life of Jesus from the Book of John. This will be a biblical study on how Jesus pursues women, then and now. We will be studying Mary, mother of Jesus, the Samaritan woman at the well, a woman, Martha, Mary of Bethany, and Mary Magdalene.

Each week will have five days of study, ideally starting on a Monday. Day 6 will serve as a catch up day, in case you miss anything or need some additional time to worship/pray/study. Day 7 will be your day of rest so that you can focus on your corporate worship experience within your local body of believers.

Secondly, we are going to be learning the Color Method of study. This method forces us to slow down and intentionally look at the same passage of Scripture, examining it in five different ways.

Here is a brief explanation of how we are going to approach the text:

You will be given one specific portion of Scripture to study each day for the week. For the first five weeks of this study, you will be repeating this process. The passages of the text have the verse numbers and extra notes taken out to make it a more natural reading experience. Each day, you will be focusing on a particular aspect of the text and will be asked to highlight with a specific color.

Here is a list of how the colors will interact with the text:

The Color Method

Green—We will highlight all names in green. This will enable us to see who the passage is talking about, who the main characters are, and who is engaging in dialogue.

Purple—We will highlight all timing words in purple. For example: then, before, later that day, noon, etc. This helps us to understand the order in which things are happening, focusing on how the people we already identified are interacting. Sometimes a passage can cover one minute, and sometimes it can cover one year. It is helpful to gather some context around the timing.

Orange—We will highlight any numbers in orange. Numbers are often significant in Scripture, helping us to recognize patterns and rhythms. Numbers help us to identify how many people are around, who the audience may be, and other important details.

Blue—We will highlight any divine acts of God, moves of the Holy Spirit, or anything supernatural with blue. It is so valuable to take the time to recognize when God is doing something only God can do. Sometimes we skip right over these parts, but the way we see the Holy Spirit work in the lives of those in Scripture can also be similar to the ways God works in our own lives.

Pink—We will highlight any verbs in pink. These are the ways in the text that either people or God are working and moving. Action is an important aspect of our faith, and it is helpful to examine how this works—the response and actions that lead to results or consequences in our study.

Yellow—We will highlight anything that God impresses upon our hearts in yellow. This can be an important aid in hearing what the Lord is speaking to us from a particular passage.

We will start out slowly as you develop the habit of looking for different aspects of Scripture. For the first five weeks, we will use one color per day as we look for specific word types, but you should always have your yellow highlighter with you, in case the Lord points out something that you want to meditate on as well.

There are a couple of reasons why we are going to approach the text this way. The very fact that you will be reading the same passage of Scripture five times will open your heart and mind to some things you may not have seen at first glance. By meditating on the same passage all week as we walk through the study itself, the hope is that each day will build upon itself as you keep the Word fresh in your heart. Lots of opportunities to journal will be provided as you move along. I would encourage you to write down what you are thinking, feeling, and learning. In those moments the Lord can work in your heart, and you will find that you are starting to *hear* from Him as He uses His Word to speak to you.

For the last week, the study will be a little different. By this point, you will have had the previous five weeks to "learn the ropes" of the Color Method. You will start to know the colors without having to refer back to the chart and possibly even begin to identify things as you read in different categories the first time you read through a passage. You will be ready for a little more.

For Week 6, you will use all five of the colors on the same passage. This is the ultimate goal with further study—to approach a passage, analyzing and reading to understand. During Week 6, I will be quiet until the last day. While Weeks 1 through 5 were about *me teaching you* how to read through a passage of Scripture, Week 6 is about *you hearing for yourself* what a passage is saying. I will, of course, add my comments toward the end of the week, because you know I can never keep my mouth shut for too long!

Another note about Week 6: Even though you will be studying the same passage of Scripture for the whole week, each day you will look through a new translation of the same passage. There are a couple of reasons for this:

1. It will force you to become even more familiar and comfortable with the entire process of the Color Method. The more practice you have with this, the more comfortable you will be when you try to use this method on your own.
2. It will also force you to use a translation you may not normally use. Throughout the study, we will use various translations. When I study on my own, I normally use the New American Standard Bible (NASB). This is because it's what I like to use and am comfortable using. Some of you may never have used that version before, and that's okay. Trying and using "new-to-you" translations can be helpful in your study.
3. Different versions may convey a new layer of meaning to your study. Because we are all coming to the table with different backgrounds and persuasions, it is impossible to predict the experience you will have as you study. However, what I have found to be true over the years is that I can be stuck on a certain passage of Scripture, but when I read it in a different version, all of a sudden it makes sense. Or it makes more sense. Or it confirms something. Or it repeats something in a way that the Lord uses. Just trust me. There is value in getting outside of your comfort zone.

There are two goals I have for you as the result of the study:

First, my hope is that by the end of our time together, you will see how Jesus interacts with women, how He speaks to them, how He calls them, and how He values them. Those things all translate to you, Sis. You are cherished by Him, and He wants you to know that.

Secondly, you will have learned how to read and understand a passage of Scripture in a way that not only makes sense, but that creates in you a desire to read the Word more. My hope is that you will have some new tools to keep you engaged in God's Word in a way that produces in you a craving for God's Word.

Well? How are you feeling? Are you ready to get started? I hope so because I am. Before we do, I just have a couple more pointers to keep you going if and when you hit any road blocks.

Sometimes there may not be any single word to highlight in a specific color, especially if the passage doesn't have something like numbers. That's okay. Don't skip it. This process is about training your brain not just to *read* the Word but to *comprehend* the Word. Even if you are not highlighting on a certain day, you are still training your brain to look for things you might otherwise have missed.

When doing the study exercises, use a *real* Bible. I know this is the age of digital everything, but there is something so sacred about getting into the Word physically. That's not to say I have never heard from the Lord using my Bible App. But…I can't remember the last time that was. More often than not, when I am physically using my Bible—highlighting, underlining, cross referencing—the Holy Spirit chooses to speak to me. Developing the discipline of getting in the Word on a regular basis is one of the reasons we are doing this study. We want to build the habit of studying the Word. I also think this sets such a good example for those around us. When others see you with Bible in hand, instead of your phone, that conveys such a powerful message.

Set aside a specific time. (This is the part where your phone comes in really handy.) I set a repeat alarm on my phone at a specific time each day, like an appointment. I would love to say that I just automatically get up early and start my day with Jesus. It's not that I wouldn't love for my life to be like that, but it isn't. I fill many roles during the day. If I am not intentional about my time, it will be taken from me by something louder in my life. I *love, love, love* studying the Word, but that doesn't mean it's automatic.

Worship. At least once a week (I do it on Saturdays), set aside some time for worship. I like to take some time after I have done the study for the week and just worship God and think about what He has been teaching me that week. It's often in those moments that He impresses on my heart the things He wants me to apply in my own life. This can be really powerful. Remember that we are not studying for the sake of acquiring knowledge—although that will happen. We are studying in order to learn from the Word and allow it to change us…so we can then go change our world.

Get engaged. You may be doing this Bible study in one of our online Bible study formats or online through a church Zoom group. One of the dangers of online interaction is, well, lack of interaction. It becomes really easy to sit back and remain quiet. In a live Bible study, you are forced to make eye contact and engage, at least somewhat. I am a social butterfly, so for me that's never an issue. But for some, online studies can be really isolating and, without accountability, may allow you to fall away quickly. Don't let that happen! Stay connected on the *She Hears* Facebook page where I can answer questions and you can discuss what you are learning with your sisters in Christ.

Keep going. Inevitably during the next six weeks, you will miss a day. It's okay. Just pick up where you left off and keep going. Some people will actually stay on track with this study because they have built it into the regular routine of their day. This is actually one of the best ways to create a good Bible study habit…by intentionally creating a margin within our busy lives to allow our hearts to hear from the Lord. By the end of the study, you will have a great habit formed, and it will make things so much easier! For some of you, this will be a struggle. You will get a day or two or six behind. It's okay. Keep going. For me, if that happens, I just double up my days until I am caught back up. It's not the best idea to try to cram all of your studying into one day. These studies are really designed for you to work through little by little, so you can digest what you are reading and learning. Allow yourself some grace, and keep going. I know that for me, I really struggle with the "all or nothing" mentality. If I get too far behind, then I tend to want to give up. Don't let that happen! The enemy wants nothing more than to steal this from you. See that tactic for what it is, and allow it to give you some new resolve to push through and stay on track. I am praying for you. You've got this, Sis!

Okay, I think we are ready. I am so excited to walk through the next month and a half with you. And you know what?

So is Jesus. Let's get started.

Be Blessed,

Rach

CHAPTER ONE

Mary, Mother of Jesus

Woman of Authority · John 2:1–11 (NASB)

When I decided to write a Bible study about the role of different women in the life of Christ, I knew I needed to begin with His mother, Mary. Since she was the primary female figure in Jesus' life, it only makes sense to start with her. However, so much is already written about Mary—entire theologies are based on her role in the life of Jesus—that the weighty task of approaching her story gave me pause. Yet I believe this is what God called me to do, so we will start fresh, like I would with any other woman in the Bible, and look at what Scripture reveals to us in our personal lives, as we seek to learn from her story. My prayer is that you will look at Mary with fresh eyes as well. Put aside any bias or preconceived ideas. Often, the evangelical church shies away from the study of the mother of Jesus, believing our focus as Christians should be on Jesus, not on Mary, so as not to allow the mother to supersede the Son. Let me remind you that Mary was a young girl—a teenager without status—when God chose her to bring His Son into the world. That fact should not be lost on us. Instead, it should inspire us, knowing that God uses ordinary people in an ordinary world to make Himself known. For that reason alone, we need to pay attention to Mary and consider the ways that *she hears* from Jesus.

Day 1

Read John 2:1–11 (NASB). As you read, underline any names in green. Use yellow to highlight any words that God impresses upon your heart.

On the third day there was a wedding in Cana of Galilee, and the mother of Jesus was there; and both Jesus and His disciples were invited to the wedding. When the wine ran out, the mother of Jesus said to Him, "They have no wine." And Jesus said to her, "What business do you have with Me, woman? My hour has not yet come." His mother said to the servants, "Whatever He tells you, do it." Now there were six stone waterpots standing there for the Jewish custom of purification, containing two or three measures each. Jesus said to them, "Fill the waterpots with water." So they filled them up to the brim. And He said to them, "Draw some out now and take it to the headwaiter." And they took it to him. Now when the headwaiter tasted the water which had become wine, and did not know where it came from (but the servants who had drawn the water knew), the headwaiter called the groom, and said to him, "Every man serves the good wine first, and when the guests are drunk, then he serves the poorer wine; but you have kept the good wine until now." This beginning of His signs Jesus did in Cana of Galilee, and revealed His glory; and His disciples believed in Him.

Use this space to write down any insights God gave you while reading through the passage.

First things first:

Our study of Mary will not focus on the season of her life that made her most famous. In fact, the portion of Scripture we will be learning from may appear to give Mary a bad rap. At first reading, many accuse Mary of being a meddling mom and applaud Jesus for standing up to her. I want to caution you, though, against taking one or two verses and basing your impression of Mary's character on them, using them as your only filter.

Has that ever happened to you? Someone formed an opinion of you based on one situation? Sometimes it's even one careless conversation. How did that make you feel?

While we are here, is there some unforgiveness or bitterness you are holding on to about that situation? If so, I would encourage you to let it go. Take a minute to think through that.

Now that we have that cleared out of the way, I want to invite you always to read the Bible through the lens of Jesus. Every time we approach the Scriptures, it is imperative that we remember two very important things:

1. We must consider each portion of Scripture in light of the Scripture as a whole. Each individual book, as well as all the chapters within that book, are part of a much larger story. All of Scripture together teaches us about who God is and His rescue plan for us as His children.

2. We must read everything through the lens of Christ. If you single out a specific verse, without reading it within the context of what we know of Jesus, then you are in danger of misunderstanding what Jesus is saying or what His intention is.

How do we accomplish those things? Well, besides being conscious of them, it is also important to look at the portion you are studying within the original context of the time it was written. Some may argue the point that the Holy Spirit can reveal what He wants us to know without additional contextual details. While that may be true, it often isn't. More often, the Holy Spirit has already revealed what He wanted us to know through His written word, and we have the responsibility of reading in a way that permits us to understand what He has already said. Before you argue with me, let's consider the following:

What version of the Bible are you reading? Is this your favorite? Do you always read this version? Do you ever switch between versions? Why do you think you make those choices?

With these thoughts in mind, let's take a look at some of the context surrounding this conversation between mother and Son in our Scripture passage for this week.

Although we will be flipping through various parts of the Bible at times, the majority of our study will come from the Book of John. I chose John because he has a unique connection to Christ. In each of these verses, you will see how John refers to himself in regard to his relationship with Jesus. Take a few minutes to look each up, writing down the common phrase in each scripture.

John 13:23 __________

John 19:26 __________

John 20:2 __________

John 21:7 __________

John 21:20 __________

How does John refer to himself? __________

When we think about relationships in our own lives, it makes sense that someone who is close to us, like a family member or close friend, might have a different perspective about us than someone who is a coworker. Not that the writers of the other gospels didn't have a close relationship with Jesus—please don't misunderstand my point—but if my sister or my daughter were to write my life story, it would have a different tone than one written by my fellow pastors. Follow me?

Keeping that in mind, we realize John may have picked up on things that the others didn't. He may have understood the motivations of Jesus in a different way. There may be details about the interactions we are studying that were not picked up by someone who had a different background or focus. In fact, all of those things are true, and entire theologies have been developed because of this unique relationship John had with Jesus. We won't get into all of that today, but I always find it helpful to understand those dynamics when I start to study a passage of Scripture. (Hint: context)

The first time we read about Mary in the Book of John, we do not find the miraculous Christmas story that we immediately think of when we refer to Mary. In fact, John doesn't mention Jesus' birth at all. However, Mary's story is still very early in John's book.

What does John call Mary when he first refers to her? Read John 2:1.

Mary is not referred to by name. Rather, John calls her "the mother of Jesus." I think this may be a clue to the relationship John had with Jesus and His family. My daughter's friends don't call me Rachael; they call me Georgia's mom or even refer to me as "Mom." I think it was intentional that John has highlighted relationship over title.

One of the things I always like to do when I study is identify the characters in a narrative. That is why I had you start your study time with names today. Looking specifically at a passage for the main characters helps you to know who was involved as well as what the overall dynamic playing out was. So this leads us to see Mary within the context of "mother."

Mothers in biblical times had a similar role to mothers today. Turn to Proverbs 1:8 and write it in the space provided.

What role does the Old Testament place on mothers?

We see here that even in the Old Testament, the mother is placed in the role of teacher. While men were the authority outside the family walls, the mother often held authority within the realm of the household and the care of children. So at some point, Mary was an authority figure to Jesus.

Think about that with me for a moment. Mary was an authority figure to Jesus. Does that strike you the way it does me? Mary had authority because God gave her authority. It wasn't her choice. It wasn't something she pursued. It was a calling God gave her. How does that make you feel when you think about it?

Think about another point with me for a moment. **The first person to have a relationship with Jesus was Mary.** Yes, Jesus was already in relationship with God, but His first human relationship was with a woman. Let's pause here for a minute.

That fact is not lost on me, and it should not be lost on you either. Nothing Jesus does is unintentional. In fact, the opposite is true. Everything Jesus does is with intention. That means that, at least on some level, Jesus Himself submitted to the authority of a woman and intentionally pursued relationship with a woman. So for women, especially those who feel called to lead within their homes, their churches, and their jobs, we see a biblical precedent set for women having a dynamic relationship with Jesus, one that has value for leadership. Jesus, even as a child, had no sin, so we can deduce that He came under the authority of His mother, a woman, willingly, without grumbling or complaining. I wonder what that means for our brothers in Christ who have rejected the idea of women being an authority, at least within some realms. My goal is not to cause division or stir up old wounds, but simply to allow for some new perspective to be brought to an old argument. **If we disallow women to lead in our churches and homes, that is a matter of personal preference, not biblical precedent.** Mary was a woman of authority.

Another aspect of Mary's character that I would like you to keep in mind is the fact that Mary was a woman of great faith. That's why she was selected by God for her mission in the first place.

What does the angel of the Lord call Mary in Luke 1:28?____________________

Favored one. The Greek word used here is *charitoō*. One of my favorite definitions of this word is "to pursue with grace and encompass with favor." God not only saw Mary as a woman of favor, but He called her a woman pursued with grace.

Mary's sincere heart and love for Yahweh touched God in such a way that she was chosen. Pursued. Given a place of honor and blessing. Not because of her position, her appearance, her finances, or her influence. She was chosen because of her faith.

Read that again. Mary's calling in life came as a result of her faith and her obedience. What does that mean for us?

For me, I was the one discarded by people who were supposed to love me. I was the one broken by someone I trusted. I was the one who carried shame so heavy that it's all I had room for in my heart. That was me. But little by little, Jesus took that all away. He took that brokenness and pain and used those cracks to allow the light to shine through. Those areas that I once tried to keep hidden are the very areas God has redeemed and used to minister to those in my life who need it the most.

When the world says no, we serve a God who says yes. God can and will redeem all things. Did you catch that? All things…if only we will let Him.

What areas of hurt do you need to surrender today? Is there something you have been holding on to that you are sensing God wants you to let go of? Take some time to reflect on that here.

____

____

____

____

____

Mary's very selection for the most important role of all time, the mother of our Savior, came as a result of her faith and her obedience. Are you in a season of not knowing your calling? Wanting to know what's next? Seeking out what God has for you?

Faith and obedience.

Day 2

Read John 2:1–11 (NASB). As you read, highlight any timing words (first, after, then, etc.) with purple. Use yellow to highlight any words that God impresses upon your heart.

On the third day there was a wedding in Cana of Galilee, and the mother of Jesus was there; and both Jesus and His disciples were invited to the wedding. When the wine ran out, the mother of Jesus said to Him, "They have no wine." And Jesus said to her, "What business do you have with Me, woman? My hour has not yet come." His mother said to the servants, "Whatever He tells you, do it." Now there were six stone waterpots standing there for the Jewish custom of purification, containing two or three measures each. Jesus said to them, "Fill the waterpots with water." So they filled them up to the brim. And He said to them, "Draw some out now and take it to the headwaiter." And they took it to him. Now when the headwaiter tasted the water which had become wine, and did not know where it came from (but the servants who had drawn the water knew), the headwaiter called the groom, and said to him, "Every man serves the good wine first, and when the guests are drunk, then he serves the poorer wine; but you have kept the good wine until now." This beginning of His signs Jesus did in Cana of Galilee, and revealed His glory; and His disciples believed in Him.

Use this space to write down any insights God gave you while reading through the passage.

Yesterday we took a look at Mary within the context of her role and relationship with Jesus. Today we are going to take a look at the setting of our story.

> *On the third day there was a wedding in Cana of Galilee, and the mother of Jesus was there; and both Jesus and His disciples were invited to the wedding.*

Today's Bible reading invites you to take a look at the timing presented in the text. Through that process, we notice something right away. This story is the very beginning of Jesus' public ministry. In fact, this is the first miracle we see Jesus perform in public, and it's significant that the miracle took place at a wedding.

Weddings within the culture of Jesus' time were a little different than how we celebrate today. Weddings in those days were celebrated with a week-long feast. Many of the close friends and all of the extended families were invited to come and celebrate. The fact that this wedding was held in Cana, a small area within Galilee, tells us that there was most likely a personal connection between the family of Jesus and the family of the bride or groom.

How does John describe the guests in the beginning of this passage?

____

____

Because John refers to Mary being present first and then adds the detail that Jesus and the disciples were there, we realize both Jesus and Mary likely had a personal connection to the family. Perhaps Mary was there out of family obligation. Mary was serving. Or perhaps she was a beloved woman who many were in relationship with and she was invited to celebrate. Jesus, who had not yet begun His public ministry, could have been there out of family obligation, either to the couple or to Mary. Obviously, this wedding was not for an unknown anonymous couple. Mary and Jesus both showed personal concern about this new marriage.

When we think about weddings and marriage in light of the broader context of the entirety of Scripture, we realize that weddings often are a symbolic reference to the relationship between God and His people.

How does God use the symbol of marriage to represent relationships in the Old Testament? Note what you learn in the following verses.

Isaiah 54:5 ____

Ezekiel 16:8 ______

Hosea 2:19 ______

In these Bible verses, we find a marriage/wedding used to represent the relationship between God and Israel.

What relationship is decribed in the New Testament? Read the verses and write your observations.

Matthew 22:1–14 ______

Matthew 25:10–13 ______

Revelation 19:7–9 ______

In these verses, we see a picture of the relationship between Christ and the Church.

Now think about this in terms of something we mentioned yesterday. Jesus does not do anything without intention. The setting He chose to use to reveal His glory for the very first time is also the same symbol we see throughout Scripture to symbolize the relationship between the Father and us. More importantly, this is the picture of how Jesus expresses His relationship between Himself and the church. Keep this in mind as we continue to study throughout the week.

What are the first words we see Mary speak in this story?

______

It is interesting that these are the first words Mary says to Jesus in this setting. At first glance, the words may appear flippant, almost like Mary is complaining. However, a couple of things are going on here that we need to understand about the culture.

Often, as we mentioned earlier, wedding feasts would last for days, with an untold number of guests. Because this was before the age of email, phones, letters, etc., hosts often found it very difficult to predict how many people would be in attendance. Families did the best they could to be prepared and tried to make sure they had enough supplies to last the entire celebration. Failure to do so would break the unwritten rules of the culture. Specifically, the act of running out of wine would bring disgrace upon the groom. What Mary saw was someone she cared about—had a personal concern for—facing a situation where they were about to be disgraced. I am sure, as most women can attest, this brought some fear, anxiety, and worry on behalf of the people she cared about. But what do we see Mary do with those emotions?

She brings them to Jesus.

They have no wine, she says.

She did not need to explain to Jesus the reasons why she was concerned. He knew.

He always knows. Our job is not to explain to Jesus all the reasons we are upset when things cause us concern. Our job is simply to bring those things to Him. There's so much to unpack there, Sis.

Just bring it to Jesus. He knows.

What is one area of your life that you hesitate to bring to Jesus? Or when you do, it's accompanied by justification and explanation about why you have so many thoughts or feelings. Does Mary's ability to take her concern to Jesus speak to you personally? Take a few minutes to let the Lord reveal to you some areas in your life that you need to bring to Him.

____

____

____

____

____

____

After Mary takes her concern to Jesus, we need to pay careful attention to how He responds to her...how He responds to us.

What does Jesus say to Mary in response?

____

Ouch. Not what you might expect. At first, this response may sting a little. If we aren't careful, we can place our own interpretation of what happened on this interaction, instead of understanding what actually happened. In fact, I have heard this small conversation used to "put women in their place" far too many times. When Mary came to Jesus with her concern, she had a very valid reason. The bride and groom running out of wine was no small deal within this culture. Jesus addresses Mary, but let's see His words for what they really are.

He is **responding,** not **reacting.**

When Jesus calls Mary "woman," this is not a sign of disrespect as it would be in our culture. In fact, this word translates as "Dear One." With that simple detail, the tone of this conversation goes from rebuff to respect. The response Jesus gives her represents a shift in their relationship. For many years, Mary served as an authority in the life of Jesus, possibly the only human authority He had after Joseph's death. Mothers were responsible for the spiritual formation of their sons. At one point, she was the one teaching the Torah to Jesus. As His mother, often her authority over Him dictated His response. It is likely that this is what she was expecting when she took her concern to Him. How we see Him respond to her is a clear picture of a turning point in their relationship.

My hour has not yet come.

What does this mean? This means that Jesus is now responding to God's authority in His life as the only authority. The timing and will of the Father now took precedence over Mary's timing and will. This shift change meant that now, only God's authority would dictate Jesus' response. Although we know God always had authority in the life of Jesus, up until this time, that authority was shared with Mary. That role and responsibility was given to Mary by God. It was also taken away by God.

Let that sink in a minute.

We all have seasons of authority that eventually we have to surrender. As a mom of teens, I am understanding this on a whole new level. But this can also apply when it comes to serving God. There are times in our lives when we are given spiritual authority for a season. That authority is only given by God, and the moment He takes that authority away, our response has to be one of surrender.

What would have happened if Mary didn't understand this? Would it have ended well for her? What happens when we try to maintain authority over something that is no longer ours to keep?

Take a few moments to reflect on what this may mean in your own life.

Mary recognizes the transfer of authority and surrenders.

What is her response in verse 5?

Mary did not take the matter into her own hands when she was met with a response she didn't expect. When she realized what the moment represented, she revealed herself as a woman of great faith as she responded. Her words to the servants were representative of her giving over any authority she had previously had over the situation. What does this mean for us?

How have you handled seasons where your authority was coming to an end? Are you in that season now? How can you recognize it when you are?

When God calls you to lay something down, are you obedient the way Mary is? What about when you get an answer you don't expect or even like, how do you respond?

Mary shows us such an example of faith. When Jesus speaks His authority to her, *she hears*. Do we follow that example?

Even when we don't know the answer or outcome, we can trust the One who does.

Day 3

Read John 2:1–11 (NASB). As you read, circle any numbers with orange. Use yellow to highlight any words that God impresses upon your heart.

On the third day there was a wedding in Cana of Galilee, and the mother of Jesus was there; and both Jesus and His disciples were invited to the wedding. When the wine ran out, the mother of Jesus said to Him, "They have no wine." And Jesus said to her, "What business do you have with Me, woman? My hour has not yet come." His mother said to the servants, "Whatever He tells you, do it." Now there were six stone waterpots standing there for the Jewish custom of purification, containing two or three measures each. Jesus said to them, "Fill the waterpots with water." So they filled them up to the brim. And He said to them, "Draw some out now and take it to the headwaiter." And they took it to him. Now when the headwaiter tasted the water which had become wine, and did not know where it came from (but the servants who had drawn the water knew), the headwaiter called the groom, and said to him, "Every man serves the good wine first, and when the guests are drunk, then he serves the poorer wine; but you have kept the good wine until now." This beginning of His signs Jesus did in Cana of Galilee, and revealed His glory; and His disciples believed in Him.

Use this space to write down any insights God gave you while reading through the passage.

Today we start our study by looking at the numbers. Sometimes understanding measurements and numbers can help us gain some perspective about a narrative. Hopefully that will help you understand some key points as we continue our study.

How many water pots were there? ______________________________

How much did each hold? ______________________________

That's basically two bathtubs worth of water. That's a lot of water, Sis.

The Jewish custom of the time was to use these water pots for religious cleansing. The fact that they were even present means this family cared about their status with God, taking care to abide by the religious expectations of the time. The words used here to describe such religious cleansing are the same descriptors used when talking about baptism. Perhaps they were part of the wedding ceremony, or maybe they were there for the guests, to allow them an opportunity to get their hearts right with God. Regardless of the reasons they were there, they were off limits. It would have been a violation of religious custom to use them for anything other than purification. Yet Jesus commands the servants to start filling them with water.

Can you place yourself in that situation for a moment?

Not only would this direction mean violating what they knew to be the custom, but put simply, it would have been a lot of work. Filling each of these pots would have taken some time.

What does Scripture say about how the servants handled this request in verse 7?

____

Not only were they obedient, but they did their job well.

When it made no sense.
When it was a lot of work.
When it was countercultural.
When it wasn't the "religious" way things had always been done.

I think that says so much to us about how we are to serve. Mary set the example by surrendering her own mind, will, and emotions, and commanding the servants in faith to follow the direction of Jesus instead. We can see by their willingness to follow this seemingly ridiculous request that Mary was a woman of authority. Her faith in Jesus, her words of surrender, and her obedience spoke to the hearts of the servants. They trusted her, and because they trusted her, they also trusted Jesus. The words of Mary led others to follow and obey Jesus. She was a woman who used her authority to point others to Christ.

What direction did Jesus give the servants after they had filled the water jars?

____

I'm not sure about you, but I have always wondered what those servants were thinking when He said this to them. They had just finished filling the containers with water. *Water!* Now Jesus was telling them to take some out and take it to the headwaiter.

How did they respond? ____

That's it. They didn't ask why. They didn't argue. They didn't wait to make sure that's really what He meant. They didn't ask for a new pitcher. They didn't ask what would happen once they did.

They took it to him.

How about you? Has God ever asked you to do something for Him that didn't seem to make any sense? At least in the physical realm? If not, can you imagine how you would feel if He did? What are some of the barriers we place in the way of obedience?

____

____

____

____

Think about this part: When Jesus told the servants to fill their pitchers, the contents of the stone water pots was still water, not wine. But the Scripture speaks of their obedience, not their complaining. Not their doubts. Not their fears. Their obedience. Sometimes the miracle happens *after* our obedience, despite what we see in the natural. Jesus does in fact transform the contents of the jars, just not in the timing we expect. Those jars sitting nearby were useless without something to fill them. Perhaps they had already been used for ceremony, but these empty jars represent so much that still holds true today. Religion is empty unless Jesus fills it. Ritual can only take care of the outside. Only Jesus can take care of the inside.

As we look to the example of the servants, we better realize why we need to serve if we love Jesus. We need to get involved in what He is doing. As we get close to Jesus, He will show us what He is doing. Often, He doesn't come right out and tell us what His plan is for our lives; instead He shows us as we are obedient to what He tells us to do. These servants were there initially to serve dinner, but being where Jesus was allowed them to be close enough to hear His voice. We begin by joining Jesus where He is...doing what He is doing. Then we obey when He tells us to do something different...whether that is serving dinner...moving water...pouring wine. Only those who listen and obey get to witness the miracle.

Have there been times where you have been tempted to quit because you didn't know what God was doing? Or it was taking longer than you thought it would? If so, reflect upon that here. Go ahead; I'll wait.

____

____

____

____

____

____

Maybe you didn't understand the direction God gave you. Maybe you are tired because it's a lot of work. Maybe you're frustrated there is still water where you are expecting wine. Don't give up. Hang in there, Sis! You may just be moments away from witnessing the miracle! Remember Mary's example...faith and obedience.

Day 4

Read John 2:1–11 (NASB). As you read, underline divine acts of God, moves of the Holy Spirit, or anything supernatural with blue. Use yellow to highlight any words that God impresses upon your heart.

On the third day there was a wedding in Cana of Galilee, and the mother of Jesus was there; and both Jesus and His disciples were invited to the wedding. When the wine ran out, the mother of Jesus said to Him, "They have no wine." And Jesus said to her, "What business do you have with Me, woman? My hour has not yet come." His mother said to the servants, "Whatever He tells you, do it." Now there were six stone waterpots standing there for the Jewish custom of purification, containing two or three measures each. Jesus said to them, "Fill the waterpots with water." So they filled them up to the brim. And He said to them, "Draw some out now and take it to the headwaiter." And they took it to him. Now when the headwaiter tasted the water which had become wine, and did not know where it came from (but the servants who had drawn the water knew), the headwaiter called the groom, and said to him, "Every man serves the good wine first, and when the guests are drunk, then he serves the poorer wine; but you have kept the good wine until now." This beginning of His signs Jesus did in Cana of Galilee, and revealed His glory; and His disciples believed in Him.

Use this space to write down any insights God gave you while reading through the passage.

Are you ready for today? It's about to get good. Today we study the supernatural. Have you ever done that before when reading the Word—specifically and intentionally looking for the things that only God can do? If not, I would encourage you to start. Soon after, what will happen is that you will see those things in your own life. The things only God can do. He is moving all around you, Sis! God wants you to be a part of what He is doing. He wants to turn your water into wine!

What happened when the servants took the water out to the headwaiter?

____

Did he know where it came from? ______________________

Who did? ______________________

Although the headwaiter was surprised and pleased by the wine, he didn't know.

The servants knew. The servants knew the miracle that had taken place because they were close enough to be part of what Jesus was doing.

And who did He use? ______________________

Jesus used the servants. They were part of the miracle. I love that! My faith and obedience are what allow me to be part of what God is doing.

Now I want to spend a little time taking a look at what this means. How does the headwaiter respond when he tastes what the servants bring him?

____

____

____

____

This passage has been taken out of context many times, so I want to point out a couple of things. This wedding was a week-long celebration, and the story takes place during the latter part of the week. The way "wine" was produced in this culture is different than how we make wine today. Often, the grape juice was boiled down to make a concentrate that could be stored, then reconstituted as needed. Because of this, wine was more like a watered-down juice drink that wasn't distilled and had very little alcohol content. It's not like everybody was drunk and Jesus then gave them more alcohol to keep partying. In fact, the opposite is true. Choice "new wine" would have been fresh, sweet juice. "New" meaning freshly made, it would not have even had time to ferment a little bit. So the taste of this "new wine" would have been sweet and unlike what they had been given before. The heart of Jesus is to set the captives free, not to encourage behavior that would lead to an addiction. Remember that we need to read everything through the lens of what we know about Jesus, who He was, and what He came to do.

What does wine represent in other parts of Scripture? Write down what you find in each of these verses.

Judges 9:13 ______________________________

Psalm 104:15 ______________________________

Ecclesiastes 9:7–9 ______________________________

Are you noticing a theme? Wine in biblical times was a metaphor for God's blessing and joy.

Turn to John 4:46 to see how this water-to-wine event is mentioned there. What does the Bible say?

____

____

He turned water into wine. That phrase is translated from the word *poieo.*

Stay with me here. Poieo means "expressing action as completed." It means to form, produce, bring about, or cause, and is spoken of as any external act manifested in the production of something tangible, obvious to the senses, *completed action.*

What else do we see wine as a symbol of? Refresh your memory by reading Luke 22:20.

____

____

____

Jesus tells them the wine is His blood, poured out for us.

Poieo. Completed action. It is finished.

Jesus is declaring His finished work on the cross with His very first manifestation of glory. Before He even starts, He is finished. And so it begins. His redemptive work on the cross will take place so our joy may be complete. So we can experience the "new wine" He has to offer. So He can cover the disgrace we didn't even know we had.

It's finished. His love, His life, poured out for us.

Does that strike you the way it strikes me? Spend some time reflecting on that here.

Day 5

Read John 2:1–11 (NASB). As you read, underline all the verbs, the action words, in pink. Use yellow to highlight any words that God impresses upon your heart.

On the third day there was a wedding in Cana of Galilee, and the mother of Jesus was there; and both Jesus and His disciples were invited to the wedding. When the wine ran out, the mother of Jesus said to Him, "They have no wine." And Jesus said to her, "What business do you have with Me, woman? My hour has not yet come." His mother said to the servants, "Whatever He tells you, do it." Now there were six stone waterpots standing there for the Jewish custom of purification, containing two or three measures each. Jesus said to them, "Fill the waterpots with water." So they filled them up to the brim. And He said to them, "Draw some out now and take it to the headwaiter." And they took it to him. Now when the headwaiter tasted the water which had become wine, and did not know where it came from (but the servants who had drawn the water knew), the headwaiter called the groom, and said to him, "Every man serves the good wine first, and when the guests are drunk, then he serves the poorer wine; but you have kept the good wine until now." This beginning of His signs Jesus did in Cana of Galilee, and revealed His glory; and His disciples believed in Him.

Use this space to write down any insights God gave you while reading through the passage.

As you reflect upon the actions of Jesus in this passage and how He worked, I want you to pay attention to a couple things. Remember what we have been learning this week as you consider the perspective of those who were there that day.

What role did Mary play in this first miracle? What example do we see in her words, her actions? Does that speak to you? How?

What role did the servants play in this first miracle? Why do you think Jesus used them? Why do you think He uses us? How does that affect how we serve?

Some work was involved in what Jesus asked the servants to do. Could He have done the work Himself? Of course He could have. God uses people because of what it will do for *us*, not because of what it will do for Him. When God chooses to use us, He helps us to see what He is doing and to understand who He is. There is such a gift in that, Sis. **The very first miracle that Jesus performed publicly was revealed to those who were serving.** The ones who know what Jesus is doing are the ones who are serving Him. They see the miracle. People who serve know that things are not what they once were, because of who Jesus is.

How does the wine being poured out at a wedding symbolize what Jesus longs to do in your own life? What does that mean for you?

The wine being poured out represents Jesus' completed action on the cross. His blood was poured out, covering our disgrace. Because He loves us, Jesus was moved to action. He covers us so no one even has to know what our lives would have been like had He not intervened.

For our final thoughts this week, I want to draw your attention to the disciples. Their activity during the course of the wedding goes unremarked until the very end of the story. What does the Scripture say about them in verse 11?

The disciples believed because of what they saw. Mary believed because of what she knew. Her voice, as a woman of authority, served as a witness to who she knew Jesus to be.

As you have studied this week, what is Jesus speaking to your heart? Just as Mary heard the words Jesus was speaking to her, I believe Jesus wants to speak some words to you. Have you been listening, Sis? What is He saying? Take some time to record that here.

As we look over this past week, my prayer is that some biblical truths have settled into your heart. Mary's role in this story, as we have studied thoroughly this week, reveals so much to us about Jesus. Let's take a look together at some key points to remember.

1. The miracle of turning water into wine is the first time Jesus performs any public miracle or sign.

I want to briefly mention here something that often gets overlooked when we simply read through the text. There is a theological concept called the "law of the first mention." To put it simply, that means there is special significance to the first time something is mentioned in Scripture. The first mention sets the tone for the rest of the same types of events that will occur later. The first time something is mentioned, it carries a little more weight. Since this is the first miracle Jesus chose to reveal in public, then we have to pay attention to the significance it carries.

After studying this miracle all week, what do you think the significance is of this first public miracle at Cana?

2. Jesus was invited.

He can't produce a miracle for us if we don't invite Him into our lives first. Have you invited Him in? Truly? To every area of your life? Take this space to write out a prayer if you need to, giving Him access to those areas you have kept from Him.

3. Take your problem to Jesus.

Mary didn't tell Jesus what to do. She didn't complain about what He didn't do. She didn't tell Him what she was planning to do and ask Him to bless it. She simply took Him the problem.

What do you need to take to Him? Have you done that? If not, spend some time doing that now.

4. Jesus calls us to radical faith and radical service.

When Mary got an unexpected response, her faith did not waiver. She acted in faith despite what she saw and heard.

No committees. No phone calls. No option. I believe the people who are obedient right away are the ones in the best possible place to experience the miracle of God. They get to see what God is doing. The servants filled their pots to the brim. They worked with excellence, not halfway. When He told them to do something radical, the faith of Mary was their example. They were obedient despite the fact that it was still water. The moment of the miracle happens in God's timing, not in Mary's…not in ours.

How have you responded when God has asked something of you that you didn't expect or understand? Do you need to talk to Him about that response?

5. He covers our disgrace.

His "choice wine" covers our disgrace in ways we don't even know. Before you were even born, your disgrace was covered by the very act of Jesus, pouring His life out for you on the cross. Are there things you are holding on to that are disgraces that you *do* know about? That you are keeping from Him? He already knows them, Sis. He already knows. It's time to deal with them. Take some time to confess them so He can cover them.

Mary. A Woman of Authority. Obedient when *she hears*.

CHAPTER TWO

Samaritan Woman at the Well

A Woman of Testimony • John 4:1–42 (NLT)

I have always loved this story from the Book of John about the Samaritan woman at the well. I was determined to learn her story in more detail, in my heart instead of just in my head. During that process, some insight came as I considered her perspective while I read about her interaction with Jesus. The more I studied, the more I realized this is not a story about a woman at a well. It's a story about Jesus at a well. The woman He meets there could easily be me, or you. As we spend some time together learning her story, let's not forget that we are part of the story. Let me remind you that you are the reason the story was written.

Day 1

Read John 4:1–42 (NLT). As you read, underline any names in green. Use yellow to highlight any words that God impresses upon your heart.

Jesus knew the Pharisees had heard that he was baptizing and making more disciples than John (though Jesus himself didn't baptize them—his disciples did). So he left Judea and returned to Galilee. He had to go through Samaria on the way. Eventually he came to the Samaritan village of Sychar, near the field that Jacob gave to his son Joseph. Jacob's well was there; and Jesus, tired from the long walk, sat wearily beside the well about noontime. Soon a Samaritan woman came to draw water, and Jesus said to her, "Please give me a drink." He was alone at the time because his disciples had gone into the village to buy some food. The woman was surprised, for Jews refuse to have anything to do with Samaritans. She said to Jesus, "You are a Jew, and I am a Samaritan woman. Why are you asking me for a drink?" Jesus replied, "If you only knew the gift God has for you and who you are speaking to, you would ask me, and I would give you living water." "But sir, you don't have a rope or a bucket," she said, "and this well is very deep. Where would you get this living water? And besides, do you think you're greater than our ancestor Jacob, who gave us this well? How can you offer better water than he and his sons and his animals enjoyed?" Jesus replied, "Anyone who drinks this water will soon become thirsty again. But those who drink the water I give will never be thirsty again. It becomes a fresh, bubbling spring within them, giving them eternal life." "Please, sir," the woman said, "give me this water! Then I'll never be thirsty again, and I won't have to come here to get water." "Go and get your husband," Jesus told her. "I don't have a husband," the woman replied. Jesus said, "You're right! You don't have a husband—for you have had five husbands, and you aren't even married to the man you're living with now. You certainly spoke the truth!" "Sir," the woman said, "you must be a prophet. So tell me, why is it that you Jews insist that Jerusalem is the only place of worship, while we Samaritans claim it is here at Mount Gerizim, where our ancestors worshiped?" Jesus replied, "Believe me, dear

woman, the time is coming when it will no longer matter whether you worship the Father on this mountain or in Jerusalem. You Samaritans know very little about the one you worship, while we Jews know all about him, for salvation comes through the Jews. But the time is coming—indeed it's here now—when true worshipers will worship the Father in spirit and in truth. The Father is looking for those who will worship him that way. For God is Spirit, so those who worship him must worship in spirit and in truth." The woman said, "I know the Messiah is coming—the one who is called Christ. When he comes, he will explain everything to us." Then Jesus told her, "I Am the Messiah!" Just then his disciples came back. They were shocked to find him talking to a woman, but none of them had the nerve to ask, "What do you want with her?" or "Why are you talking to her?" The woman left her water jar beside the well and ran back to the village, telling everyone, "Come and see a man who told me everything I ever did! Could he possibly be the Messiah?" So the people came streaming from the village to see him. Meanwhile, the disciples were urging Jesus, "Rabbi, eat something." But Jesus replied, "I have a kind of food you know nothing about." "Did someone bring him food while we were gone?" the disciples asked each other. Then Jesus explained: "My nourishment comes from doing the will of God, who sent me, and from finishing his work. You know the saying, 'Four months between planting and harvest.' But I say, wake up and look around. The fields are already ripe for harvest. The harvesters are paid good wages, and the fruit they harvest is people brought to eternal life. What joy awaits both the planter and the harvester alike! You know the saying, 'One plants and another harvests.' And it's true. I sent you to harvest where you didn't plant; others had already done the work, and now you will get to gather the harvest." Many Samaritans from the village believed in Jesus because the woman had said, "He told me everything I ever did!" When they came out to see him, they begged him to stay in their village. So he stayed for two days, long enough for many more to hear his message and believe. Then they said to the woman, "Now we believe, not just because of what you told us, but because we have heard him ourselves. Now we know that he is indeed the Savior of the world."

Use this space to write down any insights God gave you while reading through the passage.

As we start learning about the woman at the well, let's spend some time getting to know her. As we did with Mary, let's put aside any previous teaching or biases we are tempted to bring with us. Let's look at her story with fresh eyes and clear hearts. Let's read about her, approaching her story with the frame of mind that we are going to see her the way Jesus saw her. Sound good?

What are some initial thoughts you have on this? Is it hard for you to set aside preconceived ideas? Why do you think that is?

A common tendency, especially with women, is to almost like it when someone is caught up in more sin than we are. It gives us that feeling of, "Well, at least I'm not as bad as she is." Do you get what I am saying? Do you ever struggle with that? I certainly do. As much of a mess as my life might be, I find a measure of comfort that someone is worse than me. I know that thinking is messed up, but if you are honest, I bet you have had similar thoughts at some point in your life. Let's spend a little time now, getting our hearts right with God in this area. Use the space below to write out any prayers, thoughts, feelings, etc. It's okay to be honest and vulnerable here. In fact, that's what God wants, so you can experience the freedom that comes from surrendering those thoughts and attitudes to Him.

Okay, hearts clear? Good. Let's keep going.

A couple of thoughts regarding this portion of Scripture: Did you know that this is the longest recorded conversation with Jesus we have? Do you find that significant? I do. Not just because I am a talker, but because I recognize that Jesus did everything with intention. If we see that the longest conversation of Jesus ever recorded was between Jesus and a woman, we can clearly see that Jesus speaks to women. Sometimes first. At great length. He explains things to them, calls them to Himself, and allows them time to respond to Him in obedience. I love that. This concept seems so simple, yet so many overlook it. Let the concept that *she hears* from Jesus remind us that we can too.

Do you regularly hear from the Lord? If not, why do you think that is? Do you realize that you can? In fact, that's the thing Jesus longs for. You matter to Him. You are His daughter, and He loves you very much. If you need to, take a minute to reflect on that truth.

Most of the time, this story is presented with the emphasis on adultery. The woman had previously had five husbands, which is a circumstance that brings with it the heavy weight of a troubled past. Some scholars point to some ambiguity here, due to the possibility that Jesus could have been alluding to the five false religions that were practiced throughout Samaria. While we may never know the details of her exact situation, we do know there was brokenness and things didn't work out as planned. I don't know about you, but I certainly have been broken by my decisions before. Sometimes those decisions were made because they were the best options I had at the time. So many times, we don't realize the consequence and impact our decisions will make until it's too late. Before we sink to a place of condemning this woman, I think it's important to realize we all are capable of being in the same place. Without Christ, we are all broken.

I want you to take a minute to look at another passage of Scripture. Turn to Matthew 22. Take a look at verses 23-27. What are the details of that story? How many husbands did the woman have?

The very fact that this question was brought to Jesus shows us that multiple marriage situations happened sometimes. In fact, in a patriarchal society, women often needed to live with a distant relative, or in some other compromising situation, just to survive. Quite probably, this woman had suffered through the death of at least one of her husbands. Adding to that, women were not allowed to initiate divorce in that culture, but men were. If a man chose to leave the marriage, the wife was left with nothing. She would not get to keep her land, home, or belongings. Single women, in that culture, were some of the most desperate people in society.

Sycar, sometimes called Shechem, where our passage takes place, was known as a city of refuge. A city of refuge was a place where anyone who had accidentally killed someone or was responsible for a death could come, without fear of prosecution. This was one of those special cities that offered protection and mercy. I don't think it's an accident that this is the city mentioned in this story. Maybe this woman was involved in something so terrible that we can't even imagine it. And we will never know. But what we do know is that she is approached by Jesus in a season of her life when she is desperate.

Did you catch that? Desperate. Heartbroken. Abandoned. Discarded. Shamed. Guilty. Ever been there?

I have.

Have you ever been in a place where you were forced to deal with what life, or someone else, threw at you? Sometimes we suffer consequences, yes. I am not naïve to that. But sometimes we are victims of circumstances. Sometimes you do what you have to do just to survive. And this place…this place in her life, her heart rubbed raw, is the place where she meets Jesus. I don't know about you, Sis, but that's how it happened for me too. When I was in a place of absolute brokenness, that's the moment Jesus met me. He came to where I was, in the middle of my mess, and rescued me.

When was that time for you? If you haven't been there yet, think about what it would be like if you had. Maybe think about the moment you met Jesus. Was there ever a moment in your life when you were forced to make a decision between two bad options? Take some time to think through those moments here.

Do you understand what I am saying now?

This isn't just a story about a broken woman living a long time ago. This is a story about all of us, our own brokenness, and a Savior who longs to meet us where we are. It's about Him—the Redeemer—the One who can take all the things we can't control or change. He comes to that place of brokenness and enters in, in a way no one else can, to make all things new, but only if we allow Him. Let's allow Him, Sis.

As we continue on this week, I think it's so important to approach the text with this new perception of the Samaritan woman in mind. Let's put aside our judgment and see her the way Jesus sees her. Beloved. Purposed. Forgiven.

The same way He sees you.

Day 2

Read John 4:1–42 (NLT). As you read, highlight any timing words (first, after, then, etc.) with purple. Use yellow to highlight any words that God impresses upon your heart.

Jesus knew the Pharisees had heard that he was baptizing and making more disciples than John (though Jesus himself didn't baptize them—his disciples did). So he left Judea and returned to Galilee. He had to go through Samaria on the way. Eventually he came to the Samaritan village of Sychar, near the field that Jacob gave to his son Joseph. Jacob's well was there; and Jesus, tired from the long walk, sat wearily beside the well about noontime. Soon a Samaritan woman came to draw water, and Jesus said to her, "Please give me a drink." He was alone at the time because his disciples had gone into the village to buy some food. The woman was surprised, for Jews refuse to have anything to do with Samaritans. She said to Jesus, "You are a Jew, and I am a Samaritan woman. Why are you asking me for a drink?" Jesus replied, "If you only knew the gift God has for you and who you are speaking to, you would ask me, and I would give you living water." "But sir, you don't have a rope or a bucket," she said, "and this well is very deep. Where would you get this living water? And besides, do you think you're greater than our ancestor Jacob, who gave us this well? How can you offer better water than he and his sons and his animals enjoyed?" Jesus replied, "Anyone who drinks this water will soon become thirsty again. But those who drink the water I give will never be thirsty again. It becomes a fresh, bubbling spring within them, giving them eternal life." "Please, sir," the woman said, "give me this water! Then I'll never be thirsty again, and I won't have to come here to get water." "Go and get your husband," Jesus told her. "I don't have a husband," the woman replied. Jesus said, "You're right! You don't have a husband—for you have had five husbands, and you aren't even married to the man you're living with now. You certainly spoke the truth!" "Sir," the woman said, "you must be a prophet. So tell me, why is it that you Jews insist that Jerusalem is the only place of worship, while we Samaritans claim it is here at Mount Gerizim, where our ancestors worshiped?" Jesus replied, "Believe me, dear

woman, the time is coming when it will no longer matter whether you worship the Father on this mountain or in Jerusalem. You Samaritans know very little about the one you worship, while we Jews know all about him, for salvation comes through the Jews. But the time is coming—indeed it's here now—when true worshipers will worship the Father in spirit and in truth. The Father is looking for those who will worship him that way. For God is Spirit, so those who worship him must worship in spirit and in truth." The woman said, "I know the Messiah is coming—the one who is called Christ. When he comes, he will explain everything to us." Then Jesus told her, "I Am the Messiah!" Just then his disciples came back. They were shocked to find him talking to a woman, but none of them had the nerve to ask, "What do you want with her?" or "Why are you talking to her?" The woman left her water jar beside the well and ran back to the village, telling everyone, "Come and see a man who told me everything I ever did! Could he possibly be the Messiah?" So the people came streaming from the village to see him. Meanwhile, the disciples were urging Jesus, "Rabbi, eat something." But Jesus replied, "I have a kind of food you know nothing about." "Did someone bring him food while we were gone?" the disciples asked each other. Then Jesus explained: "My nourishment comes from doing the will of God, who sent me, and from finishing his work. You know the saying, 'Four months between planting and harvest.' But I say, wake up and look around. The fields are already ripe for harvest. The harvesters are paid good wages, and the fruit they harvest is people brought to eternal life. What joy awaits both the planter and the harvester alike! You know the saying, 'One plants and another harvests.' And it's true. I sent you to harvest where you didn't plant; others had already done the work, and now you will get to gather the harvest." Many Samaritans from the village believed in Jesus because the woman had said, "He told me everything I ever did!" When they came out to see him, they begged him to stay in their village. So he stayed for two days, long enough for many more to hear his message and believe. Then they said to the woman, "Now we believe, not just because of what you told us, but because we have heard him ourselves. Now we know that he is indeed the Savior of the world."

Use this space to write down any insights God gave you while reading through the passage.

Today as we continue our study of the Samaritan woman at the well, I want to back up a little to take a look at the Samaritan culture itself. If we study that aspect, I believe it will help us understand things from a little different perspective.

Samaritans (their name meaning "keepers of the law") thought they were doing things right. I can identify with that because there have been times in my life when I *thought* I was doing things right. Not until I met Jesus did I realize how wrong I was. The people were not called Samaritans because they were from Samaria but because they worked hard to follow the laws they thought they needed to obey in order to be right in the sight of God. This wasn't exactly easy, however, because Samaritans practiced a mix of religions. To explain this further, let's flip back to the Old Testament for a bit. Turn with me to 2 Kings 17 and read through it.

What groups of people were settled in Samaria? (vs 24)

I know the passage is long and wordy, but I would encourage you to read about what's going on in this time of Israel's history, both in chapter 17 as well as the surrounding chapters. A quick summary for those of you who saw how long it was and just skipped down to verse 24:

The Northern Kingdom, Israel, had been disobedient to God by allowing all sorts of idol worship and evil to corrupt the land. Things like child sacrifice and temple prostitutes were the norm. As a result, after years of disobedience and extra chances, God allowed the people of Israel to be captured and taken away by the Assyrians. The Assyrians, you may remember from your childhood Sunday school class, were the bad guys Jonah was avoiding when he got swallowed by the whale. Different period of history, but same guys.

They were known as merciless, to say the least. The Assyrians left some of the poorest, and who they considered the most worthless, Israelites behind. After a period of exile, the Assyrians brought back captives from other lands to occupy Israel. The hope was that by having a mixture of people from various lands, they would avoid any kind of revolt based on unity. (Side note: I think even that right there speaks to the power found in community.)

Regardless, something really interesting happened there. We will pick up in verse 24:

> *The king of Assyria brought people from Babylon, Kuthah, Avva, Hamath, and Sepharvaim and settled them in the towns of Samaria to replace the Israelites. They took over Samaria and lived in its towns. When they first lived there, they did not worship the LORD; so he sent lions among them and they killed some of the people.* (NIV®)

Hold up. Did you catch that? Lions. The people who resettled the land worshiped other gods instead of Yahweh. This was the reason why the original people of the land were punished in the first place. So God sent a plague of lions to remind these people to Whom this land belonged. Things grew so bad that word got back to the King of Assyria. Picking up in vs 26:

> *It was reported to the king of Assyria: "The people you deported and resettled in the towns of Samaria do not know what the god of that country requires. He has sent lions among them, which are killing them off, because the people do not know what he requires." Then the king of Assyria gave this order: "Have one of the priests you took captive from Samaria go back to live there and teach the people what the god of the land requires." So one of the priests who had been exiled from Samaria came to live in Bethel and taught them how to worship the LORD.* (NIV®)

Seriously? Are you following this? It sounds like a movie. In fact, I would certainly pay money to see this played out on the big screen. The king gets word of what is going on, so he sends back a priest he had captured to teach them how to follow Yahweh. Now before you scratch your head, let me explain something else. The religious culture of the Assyrians was polytheistic. More so, any "god" that had any measure of power, according to the people, was celebrated, basically in a "the more the merrier" type of scenario. They wanted to cover all their bases, so to speak. The king sent a priest to deal with this little lion problem, and from all we can tell, it worked. Yahweh had a plan to make His name known as the God of Israel, despite the human interventions going on. You would think that would have been enough to straighten the people of Samaria out. But nope. Watch what happens next in vs 29.

Nevertheless, each national group made its own gods in the several towns where they settled, and set them up in the shrines the people of Samaria had made at the high places. (NIV®)

Now we have four groups of people: (1) a group of people serving Yahweh mixed into (2) a group of people that serve Yahweh *and* all these other false gods. We also have (3) a group of people who *only* serve false gods. And they all mixed together with (4) the "worthless" and poor Jews that had been initially left behind. These people became the group of people that Scripture refers to as Samaritans.

I know this is a lot.... Stay with me, Sis. I promise it will be worth it.

Now the Jews, the ones who had remained faithful to Yahweh, were a group that worked hard to keep themselves from being tainted so as to not become "unclean." They saw the Samaritans as anything but clean.

At this point in Israel's history, the Samaritans and the Jews did not get along at all. In fact, the tensions were so high that if the Jews had to travel from Galilee to Judea, they typically would cross the Jordan River and travel alongside it, even crossing back and forth a couple of times, in order to avoid going through Samaria.

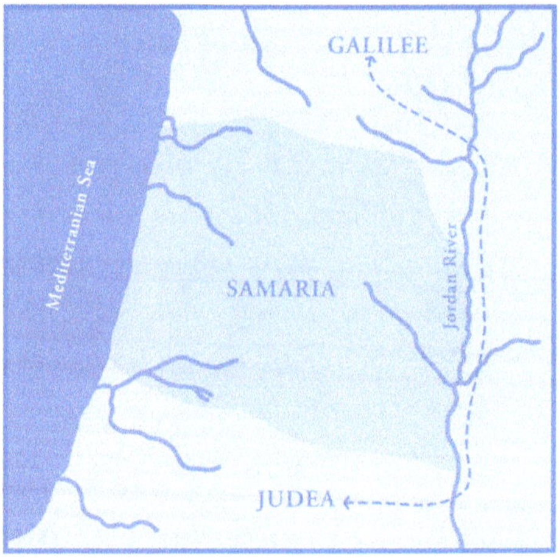

Have you ever gone the long way in order to avoid the "bad part of town"? That's kind of what was going on here. The Jews saw Samaria as a place that would defile them even if they just walked through.

Are you starting to get a better picture now? Tomorrow we will put all of this together in light of our story. But for now, I want you to spend some time in prayer, maybe thinking about some people in your life that you avoid. Could it be God is wanting to start working with you in that area? Perhaps He wants to soften your heart a little so that if the opportunity came to reach them with the gospel, your heart would be in a posture of obedience and readiness instead of judgment and avoidance. I know this is hard stuff, Sis, but trust me, it's worth it. In the next couple of days, we are going to see this all start to come together, but I want you to approach that time with some of this stuff laid bare. It's the only way to allow those spaces to heal.

Day 3

Read John 4:1–42 (NLT). As you read, circle any numbers with orange. Use yellow to highlight any words that God impresses upon your heart.

Jesus knew the Pharisees had heard that he was baptizing and making more disciples than John (though Jesus himself didn't baptize them—his disciples did). So he left Judea and returned to Galilee. He had to go through Samaria on the way. Eventually he came to the Samaritan village of Sychar, near the field that Jacob gave to his son Joseph. Jacob's well was there; and Jesus, tired from the long walk, sat wearily beside the well about noontime. Soon a Samaritan woman came to draw water, and Jesus said to her, "Please give me a drink." He was alone at the time because his disciples had gone into the village to buy some food. The woman was surprised, for Jews refuse to have anything to do with Samaritans. She said to Jesus, "You are a Jew, and I am a Samaritan woman. Why are you asking me for a drink?" Jesus replied, "If you only knew the gift God has for you and who you are speaking to, you would ask me, and I would give you living water." "But sir, you don't have a rope or a bucket," she said, "and this well is very deep. Where would you get this living water? And besides, do you think you're greater than our ancestor Jacob, who gave us this well? How can you offer better water than he and his sons and his animals enjoyed?" Jesus replied, "Anyone who drinks this water will soon become thirsty again. But those who drink the water I give will never be thirsty again. It becomes a fresh, bubbling spring within them, giving them eternal life." "Please, sir," the woman said, "give me this water! Then I'll never be thirsty again, and I won't have to come here to get water." "Go and get your husband," Jesus told her. "I don't have a husband," the woman replied. Jesus said, "You're right! You don't have a husband—for you have had five husbands, and you aren't even married to the man you're living with now. You certainly spoke the truth!" "Sir," the woman said, "you must be a prophet. So tell me, why is it that you Jews insist that Jerusalem is the only place of worship, while we Samaritans claim it is here at Mount Gerizim, where our ancestors worshiped?" Jesus replied, "Believe me, dear

woman, the time is coming when it will no longer matter whether you worship the Father on this mountain or in Jerusalem. You Samaritans know very little about the one you worship, while we Jews know all about him, for salvation comes through the Jews. But the time is coming—indeed it's here now—when true worshipers will worship the Father in spirit and in truth. The Father is looking for those who will worship him that way. For God is Spirit, so those who worship him must worship in spirit and in truth." The woman said, "I know the Messiah is coming—the one who is called Christ. When he comes, he will explain everything to us." Then Jesus told her, "I Am the Messiah!" Just then his disciples came back. They were shocked to find him talking to a woman, but none of them had the nerve to ask, "What do you want with her?" or "Why are you talking to her?" The woman left her water jar beside the well and ran back to the village, telling everyone, "Come and see a man who told me everything I ever did! Could he possibly be the Messiah?" So the people came streaming from the village to see him. Meanwhile, the disciples were urging Jesus, "Rabbi, eat something." But Jesus replied, "I have a kind of food you know nothing about." "Did someone bring him food while we were gone?" the disciples asked each other. Then Jesus explained: "My nourishment comes from doing the will of God, who sent me, and from finishing his work. You know the saying, 'Four months between planting and harvest.' But I say, wake up and look around. The fields are already ripe for harvest. The harvesters are paid good wages, and the fruit they harvest is people brought to eternal life. What joy awaits both the planter and the harvester alike! You know the saying, 'One plants and another harvests.' And it's true. I sent you to harvest where you didn't plant; others had already done the work, and now you will get to gather the harvest." Many Samaritans from the village believed in Jesus because the woman had said, "He told me everything I ever did!" When they came out to see him, they begged him to stay in their village. So he stayed for two days, long enough for many more to hear his message and believe. Then they said to the woman, "Now we believe, not just because of what you told us, but because we have heard him ourselves. Now we know that he is indeed the Savior of the world."

Use this space to write down any insights God gave you while reading through the passage.

Today I want to start by having you look again at the map from yesterday. I want that image fresh in your mind as we begin to study. That will help you understand some pivotal points as we analyze the text.

As we look at the beginning of the scripture we are studying this week, we will see that Jesus is starting in Judea and traveling to Galilee. I want you to pay special attention to verse 4.

He **had to go** *through Samaria on the way.* (emphasis mine)

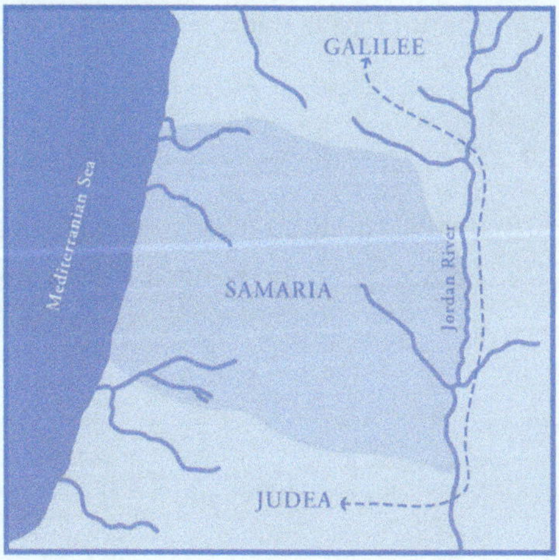

Now, you may have already picked up on some of this as we studied yesterday. The Word says he *had to go.* In the past, when I read that, I always thought it was a travel directive. Like, you have to turn left in order to get somewhere. But in this case, it's the opposite of what you might think. Yesterday, we spent the entire day learning about this rift between the Samaritans and the Jews. Not only is it *not* true that Jesus had to go through Samaria directionally, going that way was also actually counter-cultural. I want you to consider something with me—the phrase "had to go."

That phrase comes from the word *dei***.** This word dei means: a directive coming from God as part of His plan. We see that phrase used elsewhere in Scripture.

Look up Matthew 16:21 and write it in the space below. Highlight the words you think may be the same phrase.

In my Bible, the verse reads "he must go," but the phrase is the same as the one used in John 4:4. The same word is used when talking about how Jesus *had to go* to the cross. There was never an option not to go. Rather, it was always part of the plan—God's plan. How does that change anything? Well, if we think in terms of what was about to happen in our story, it means God had a plan for Jesus to be at the well when the woman came. Jesus didn't just "happen" to be traveling through. The route wasn't a shortcut to Galilee. It wasn't the typical travel route for the Jews Jesus was traveling with. Jesus wasn't going because the Samaritan woman invited Him. Are you with me?

Jesus' pursuit of her was not accidental; it was intentional. Jesus, breaking the cultural and religious traditions of the time, sought out this woman. He was there, waiting for her. His pursuit of you is intentional too.

Yes. You.

Take a minute if you need to. You may want to journal your thoughts about the fact that God pursues you. When I understood this fully for the first time, it changed things for me. It still does. Go ahead, I'll wait.

Okay, now I want to show you something about the location of this conversation between Jesus and the Samaritan woman.

We know that Jesus, despite cultural and religious norms, has pursued this woman with intention, and He chooses a particular place for their encounter.

Where is that? ____

In a patriarchal society, especially one that was familiar with the Torah, John's audience would understand a well to mean something a little bit different than the well you and I are familiar with. To demonstrate my point, I want to show you some examples from Scripture.

Whose well was this? What happened there? Look up this story in Genesis 29:1–14. Write down any thoughts and insights you gain.

Now let's look at another story of a well. Read through Genesis 24, starting at verse 9. What happened at that well? Write down any thoughts and insights you gain.

Okay. One more. Read through Exodus 2, starting at verse 15. What happened at that well? Write down any thoughts and insights you gain.

Well… (Like what I did there?) What did you come up with? What does a well often set the scene for? We see that Jacob and Rachel, Isaac and Rebekah, and Moses and Zipporah all started their relationships at a well. In this culture, these stories were ones the Samaritans would have known. Remember, though there were disagreements about how the law was kept, Samaritans did, in fact, keep the law. They knew the Torah. The well was often the center of the social scene in so many respects. Throughout Scripture, the well hints at a repeated "type scene," which basically just means that people start the path to marriage at a well. What does that mean for us and our Samaritan woman? Marriage may not have been her intention or purpose in going to the well that day, but we know this fact was not lost on Jesus. Now, before you get all upset because you think I am insinuating something, let me just say that I am not. Stick with me here.

The word for "well" that is used here is *pēgē,* which means a well fed by a spring.

This well that served as a meeting place for Jesus and the unnamed Samaritan woman was not just a place to draw water from a cistern. Instead, it was a *source of supply* for their community. In addition to typically being a setting for betrothal, the well was representative of everything that sustained life in that culture. Relationships were developed and cultivated at the well. If we think of what the well would have represented to John's readers, clearly this meeting spot was intentional on Jesus' part.

Jesus would become the source of supply.

He would become the bridegroom of the Church, as the Samaritans came to faith in Jesus as the Christ.

Sis, I want you to realize this.

Jesus pursues us with intention.

It's who He is. He seeks us out. Often times, at the exact moment when we don't want to be found. That's how much He loves us. Do you get it now? Spend some time reflecting on what this all means for you in your own life.

And Sis?

He's never going to stop.

Day 4

Read John 4:1–42 (NLT). As you read, underline divine acts of God, moves of the Holy Spirit, anything supernatural with blue. Use yellow to highlight any words that God impresses upon your heart.

Jesus knew the Pharisees had heard that he was baptizing and making more disciples than John (though Jesus himself didn't baptize them—his disciples did). So he left Judea and returned to Galilee. He had to go through Samaria on the way. Eventually he came to the Samaritan village of Sychar, near the field that Jacob gave to his son Joseph. Jacob's well was there; and Jesus, tired from the long walk, sat wearily beside the well about noontime. Soon a Samaritan woman came to draw water, and Jesus said to her, "Please give me a drink." He was alone at the time because his disciples had gone into the village to buy some food. The woman was surprised, for Jews refuse to have anything to do with Samaritans. She said to Jesus, "You are a Jew, and I am a Samaritan woman. Why are you asking me for a drink?" Jesus replied, "If you only knew the gift God has for you and who you are speaking to, you would ask me, and I would give you living water." "But sir, you don't have a rope or a bucket," she said, "and this well is very deep. Where would you get this living water? And besides, do you think you're greater than our ancestor Jacob, who gave us this well? How can you offer better water than he and his sons and his animals enjoyed?" Jesus replied, "Anyone who drinks this water will soon become thirsty again. But those who drink the water I give will never be thirsty again. It becomes a fresh, bubbling spring within them, giving them eternal life." "Please, sir," the woman said, "give me this water! Then I'll never be thirsty again, and I won't have to come here to get water." "Go and get your husband," Jesus told her. "I don't have a husband," the woman replied. Jesus said, "You're right! You don't have a husband—for you have had five husbands, and you aren't even married to the man you're living with now. You certainly spoke the truth!" "Sir," the woman said, "you must be a prophet. So tell me, why is it that you Jews insist that Jerusalem is the only place of worship, while we Samaritans claim it is here at Mount Gerizim, where our ancestors worshiped?" Jesus replied, "Believe me, dear

woman, the time is coming when it will no longer matter whether you worship the Father on this mountain or in Jerusalem. You Samaritans know very little about the one you worship, while we Jews know all about him, for salvation comes through the Jews. But the time is coming—indeed it's here now—when true worshipers will worship the Father in spirit and in truth. The Father is looking for those who will worship him that way. For God is Spirit, so those who worship him must worship in spirit and in truth." The woman said, "I know the Messiah is coming—the one who is called Christ. When he comes, he will explain everything to us." Then Jesus told her, "I Am the Messiah!" Just then his disciples came back. They were shocked to find him talking to a woman, but none of them had the nerve to ask, "What do you want with her?" or "Why are you talking to her?" The woman left her water jar beside the well and ran back to the village, telling everyone, "Come and see a man who told me everything I ever did! Could he possibly be the Messiah?" So the people came streaming from the village to see him. Meanwhile, the disciples were urging Jesus, "Rabbi, eat something." But Jesus replied, "I have a kind of food you know nothing about." "Did someone bring him food while we were gone?" the disciples asked each other. Then Jesus explained: "My nourishment comes from doing the will of God, who sent me, and from finishing his work. You know the saying, 'Four months between planting and harvest.' But I say, wake up and look around. The fields are already ripe for harvest. The harvesters are paid good wages, and the fruit they harvest is people brought to eternal life. What joy awaits both the planter and the harvester alike! You know the saying, 'One plants and another harvests.' And it's true. I sent you to harvest where you didn't plant; others had already done the work, and now you will get to gather the harvest." Many Samaritans from the village believed in Jesus because the woman had said, "He told me everything I ever did!" When they came out to see him, they begged him to stay in their village. So he stayed for two days, long enough for many more to hear his message and believe. Then they said to the woman, "Now we believe, not just because of what you told us, but because we have heard him ourselves. Now we know that he is indeed the Savior of the world."

Use this space to write down any insights God gave you while reading through the passage.

Today our study picks up at the moment that the Samaritan woman and Jesus finally meet. What were the first words Jesus said to her?

Jesus, having pursued this location and this conversation with intention, finally gets the chance to speak to this woman. The first thing that happens when they meet?

He asks something of her.

The moment we meet Jesus, He asks something of us too. Don't miss this part, Sis. This isn't a bossy man demanding something from a servant girl. And please don't misunderstand, thinking I am a heretic. I know that salvation from Jesus is a free gift. But in order to receive that gift, we have to give Him what we are holding on to. Our hands need to be empty in order to take something.

Read through this section again. How does she respond to Jesus?

She immediately responds with an argument. *But you don't have a rope or a bucket.*

I know that on this side of things, it's easy to think she is being foolish. But Sis, we do the same thing. The moment we meet Jesus, not even realizing who He is yet, we argue with Him when He asks us to lay down the thing that is keeping us from Him.

Our hands aren't empty to receive His free gift, because they are filled with things that we refuse to lay down. You may be thinking right now of all the things you just can't lay down. We all have this blind spot initially, where we can't see in the physical how Jesus can meet our needs in the spiritual.

I can't lay down unforgiveness.
I can't lay down abuse.
I can't lay down fear.
I can't lay down this sin.

I get it. And you're right, you can't. Neither could she.

Let's keep going for a moment.

Jesus, knowing this about her, and about us, responds with a promise. Re-read verses 13–15.

> *Jesus replied, "Anyone who drinks this water will soon become thirsty again. But those who drink the water I give will never be thirsty again. It becomes a fresh, bubbling spring within them, giving them eternal life."*
>
> *"Please, sir," the woman said, "give me this water! Then I'll never be thirsty again, and I won't have to come here to get water."*

Most of us, when we hear of the freedom that comes from knowing Christ, respond with, "Yes! I want that!" We just don't quite know how to get it—how to lay those things down and not pick them back up. Keep reading, verses 16–18.

> *"Go and get your husband," Jesus told her. "I don't have a husband," the woman replied. Jesus said, "You're right! You don't have a husband—for you have had five husbands, and you aren't even married to the man you're living with now. You certainly spoke the truth!"*

Now, we started Day 1 of our study this week with a conversation about this very moment. We don't know exactly what her life experience had been, but what we do know is that there is a place of pain and shame that Jesus addresses here. I want you to realize something. This isn't a "gotcha" moment—it's a "give Me" moment. Jesus addresses her situation because He wants to work through it. He wants her to see that regardless of what she thinks she is hiding, He knows. Her response? A religious argument. I've done that before too.

"I prayed about this before, nothing happened. I went to church, nothing happened. I even tried reading my Bible, nothing happened. The mess in my life was still there." Or "I tried to stop, but I can't."

Jesus' response? Skip down to verse 26. What does He call Himself?

He responds to her by declaring who He is—the Messiah. That name, Messiah, means "one who is anointed to deliver."

And what does anointed mean? It means set apart for a specific task. The Jewish culture anointed their leaders, much like we do. We have children's pastors and youth pastors, preachers and elders—people who are set apart to do a job they are assigned to do.

Jesus was set apart as deliverer. It's who He is. But it goes beyond that—the word "deliverer." It doesn't just mean escape or rescue like you may think. It means "to snatch away."

Do you see it, Sis? Jesus wants to snatch away from you the very thing you feel like you can't lay down.

It's who He is. It's what He was sent here to do.

His name, Messiah, is not just a promise for *one* day—it's a promise for right now. Right now!

I want you to understand who He is saying He is. If you only knew. It's not about your ability to give it away or lay it down. It's about the very job He came to this earth to do. He knows what you hide from everyone else. That's the thing He wants you to give Him.

And if you can't? He wants to snatch it away from you. To redeem you. To restore you. Jesus was set apart to deliver you from what you cannot hand over yourself.

Do you need a minute? I thought you might. Take some time to reflect on this truth. Write down some things you have struggled to give to Him. Maybe even some things you need Him to snatch away. I know I am asking you to be vulnerable right now, but that's because I want you to have freedom, Sis. And besides, He already knows what it is.

How ya doing? You still with me? One more thing. Turn to 2 Peter 2:9, and write it in the space below.

Did you catch that? Jesus knows how to rescue godly people from their trials.

He knows what He is doing.

I wish I could say this is a one-and-done scenario, and now that you have surrendered this thing, it would just be over. But it doesn't work that way. You see, there is a reason Jesus is talking about living water in this scene.

The word that is used here when the scripture talks about taking a drink is the word *pineto*. That word means "continuing or repeated."

Do you see where I am going with this? Freedom from this thing, whatever it is for you... Shame. Fear. Anxiety. Sin.

Freedom only comes from regular interaction with the One who can take it away. Thirst for peace and freedom is only quenched by the Source. It's not a one time, "I prayed that prayer" scenario. It's not about church. It's about you and Jesus—allowing Him to "snatch away" that thing you are desperate to get rid of. Daily. Did you hear me? *Daily.*

Jesus wants to take what you are holding on to. But you have to let Him.

Day 5

Read John 4:1–42 (NLT). As you read, underline all the verbs, the action words, in pink. Use yellow to highlight any words that God impresses upon your heart.

Jesus knew the Pharisees had heard that he was baptizing and making more disciples than John (though Jesus himself didn't baptize them—his disciples did). So he left Judea and returned to Galilee. He had to go through Samaria on the way. Eventually he came to the Samaritan village of Sychar, near the field that Jacob gave to his son Joseph. Jacob's well was there; and Jesus, tired from the long walk, sat wearily beside the well about noontime. Soon a Samaritan woman came to draw water, and Jesus said to her, "Please give me a drink." He was alone at the time because his disciples had gone into the village to buy some food. The woman was surprised, for Jews refuse to have anything to do with Samaritans. She said to Jesus, "You are a Jew, and I am a Samaritan woman. Why are you asking me for a drink?" Jesus replied, "If you only knew the gift God has for you and who you are speaking to, you would ask me, and I would give you living water." "But sir, you don't have a rope or a bucket," she said, "and this well is very deep. Where would you get this living water? And besides, do you think you're greater than our ancestor Jacob, who gave us this well? How can you offer better water than he and his sons and his animals enjoyed?" Jesus replied, "Anyone who drinks this water will soon become thirsty again. But those who drink the water I give will never be thirsty again. It becomes a fresh, bubbling spring within them, giving them eternal life." "Please, sir," the woman said, "give me this water! Then I'll never be thirsty again, and I won't have to come here to get water." "Go and get your husband," Jesus told her. "I don't have a husband," the woman replied. Jesus said, "You're right! You don't have a husband—for you have had five husbands, and you aren't even married to the man you're living with now. You certainly spoke the truth!" "Sir," the woman said, "you must be a prophet. So tell me, why is it that you Jews insist that Jerusalem is the only place of worship, while we Samaritans claim it is here at Mount Gerizim, where our ancestors worshiped?" Jesus replied, "Believe me, dear woman, the time is coming when it will no longer matter whether you worship the Father on this mountain or in Jerusalem. You Samaritans know very little about the one you worship, while we Jews know all about him, for salvation comes through the Jews. But the time is coming—indeed it's here now—when true worshipers will worship the Father in spirit and in truth. The Father is looking for those who will worship him that way. For God is Spirit, so those who worship him must worship in spirit and in truth." The woman said, "I know the Messiah is coming—the one who is called Christ. When he comes, he will explain everything to us." Then Jesus told her, "I AM the Messiah!" Just then his disciples came back. They were shocked to find him talking to a woman, but none of them had the nerve to ask, "What do you want with her?" or "Why are you talking to her?" The woman left her water jar beside the well and ran back to the village, telling everyone, "Come and see a man who told me everything I ever did! Could he possibly be the Messiah?" So the people came streaming from the village to see him. Meanwhile, the disciples were urging Jesus, "Rabbi, eat something." But Jesus replied, "I have a kind of food you know nothing about." "Did someone bring him food while we were gone?" the disciples asked each other. Then Jesus explained: "My nourishment comes from doing the will of God, who sent me, and from finishing his work. You know the saying, 'Four months between planting and harvest.' But I say, wake up and look around. The fields are already ripe for harvest. The harvesters are paid good wages, and the fruit they harvest is people brought to eternal life. What joy awaits both the planter and the harvester alike! You know the saying, 'One plants and another harvests.' And it's true. I sent you to harvest where you didn't plant; others had already done the work, and now you will get to gather the harvest." Many Samaritans from the village believed in Jesus because the woman had said, "He told me everything I ever did!" When they came out to see him, they begged him to stay in their village. So he stayed for two days, long enough for many more to hear his message and believe. Then they said to the woman, "Now we believe, not just because of what you told us, but because we have heard him ourselves. Now we know that he is indeed the Savior of the world."

Use this space to write down any insights God gave you while reading through the passage.

As we finish up our week, I want to review a couple of aspects we covered. We are going to start with the water.

We realize our need for a Savior only after we realize our stain from sin. The grace that meets us becomes the very thing that sustains us. If we think in terms of cultural context, thirst is not the only thing that the living water remedies. The Samaritan woman also needs the cleansing she has been longing for, for years.

Women who were divorced would not have been permitted near any of the ritual bath-houses. Even though she may have physically cleaned herself, likely with water from this very well, she could not have gone through a purification bath, perhaps for several years. Remember, Samaritans were keepers of the law. This was one aspect of the law that the Jews and the Samaritans agreed upon. So if she was just cleaning herself up, she would have had to return to this well often. But try as she might, she would not be able to escape the stain of her sin, in the religious sense.

Jesus was offering her something no one else could give.

What happens when she finally realizes this? Read verse 28–29. How did she respond?

As the woman receives what she is looking for, completely overcome with what she has received, she rushes off to share the news, forgetting her water pot behind. We see a woman, who previously had isolated herself from her community, receiving grace in a powerful way. So powerful, in fact, that she forgot the very reason she approached the well in the first place.

I want you to spend a little time reviewing the different aspects of water in some other places in Scripture. Look up the following verses, and make a few notes about what you learn:

Exodus 17:5–6 ______________________________

____

____

Numbers 20:1–11 ______________________________

____

____

Numbers 21:16–18 ______________________________

____

____

Jeremiah 2:13 ______________________________

____

____

Throughout the Bible, living water represents the spiritual life, the Spirit of God, and a symbol of Jesus as Messiah.

In what area of your own life are you in need of some "living water"? What areas are parched and dry because you haven't been going to the Source? Sis, He wants to quench that thirst. He wants you to know that you don't ever have to be dry again. Spend some time in prayer, considering what this means in your own life.

____

____

____

Once the Samaritan woman comes to this place in her heart, she is overcome with the desire to go and tell everyone she knows this incredibly good news.

I want you to pay attention to what happens next. It is especially important.

Even the disciples were surprised at how Jesus broke the social and cultural rules. They had spent so much time with Him that you might think they would have realized by now that His heart to reach people went beyond the boundaries they had been taught to respect. In fact, He came to turn that entire system upside down, to offer grace in a completely radical way. What we realize with her reaction is that *an authentic interaction with Jesus gives us freedom from that which we can't lay down on our own.*

I am not sure if that means to you what it means to me. When I look back over my own life, my memory rests on an area where I struggled with a form of addiction. Try as I might, I was never quite able to give it up. It's not that I didn't want to or hadn't tried. It was just that, in times of stress, I would pick that bad habit right back up again. It wasn't until I surrendered my heart, and not just my life, to Jesus that I finally forgot about the very thing I had held on to for so long. In fact, I didn't even realize I had been delivered until I started thinking about this concept. My interaction at the well—my relationship with Jesus—became the authentic and repeated craving of my heart. Jesus replaced the addictive thing in my life, and I didn't even miss it or realize I no longer needed it. It can be that way for you too, Sis.

Who is this woman at the well? She is me. She is us. And Jesus longs to do for us what He did for her.

I don't know what you are holding on to today, but I do know this. Freedom starts with an authentic interaction with Jesus, and that's where it continues. If you only knew who He is. The Messiah. The Deliverer. The Restorer. It's not about today. It's about every day. Take a little time if you need it. This can feel heavy, I know, but it doesn't have to. This can be the first step in your healing. Allow Him to do that for you, Sis. He wants that for you. And so do I.

A couple more things before we close out this week. Some encouragement is here for you that I want to make sure you see.

Our Samaritan woman, who by now I hope you have a different perspective on, was the first evangelist sent to the Gentiles that we ever see in the gospel. Jesus breaks barriers of gender and religion, culture and race with His interaction with her. But layered upon the broken past of this anonymous woman is a calling and commissioning that many women today do not take up because of barriers of gender and religion, race and culture. Do you see the irony here? Jesus is not the one who disqualifies women for evangelistic leadership. She may have seemed an unlikely candidate to be chosen, yet as followers of Christ, we serve a God who says yes when everyone else says no. Isn't that amazing? There's some power there, Sis. If you sense a calling in this area, if Jesus has put that in your heart, don't let anyone else tell you differently.

Jesus clarifies our worthiness to answer His call based on who He is, not who we are. Amen?!

And here is my final point in this week's story:

The disciples had been down in town for quite some time, yet we only see the townspeople coming to Jesus as a result of *her* words, not the disciples'. It's like that for us too. You see, God has perfectly selected *you* for *your* community, for *your* circle of influence. Why?

You have a message *no one else* can speak.

Because of her testimony, the people of Samaria came to Jesus. Prior to her interaction with Jesus, this woman had been rejected in her community for her past. Yet she is chosen to share with her community this message of what Christ did within her, despite her past. Her interaction with Jesus becomes her testimony, and this interaction is all she needs. Out of the overflow of her heart, she shares Jesus with anyone who will listen.

That's kind of how it happened for me too. That's why I am writing now. I can't *not* tell you. I *have* to. I *have* to share with you what Jesus taught me at the well.

And He wants to use you to tell your own story. Take a couple of minutes to reflect on what that means for you. Who might God want you to share His "living water" with? Is there someone He is bringing to mind? If so, write down their name and pray for them.

CHAPTER THREE

Woman

A Woman of Forgiveness • John 8:1–11 (NASB)

This week, we will be taking a look at a story from the Book of John that is on the heavy side. We will be studying the woman caught in adultery in John Chapter 8. Most studies on this portion of Scripture are entitled, "Sinful Woman" or "Adulterous Woman." While that is certainly an accurate description of what is happening in this passage, I decided to simply call this week, "Woman." I don't know about you, but plenty of labels could be attached to my name. Jealous. Fearful. Revengeful. Ashamed. We all have moments in our lives, our hidden lives, that we are not proud of. As we study the grace and forgiveness that come from Jesus, my hope is that we will begin to identify ourselves by His words of restoration in our lives rather than by the labels our sin places on us. Jesus says we are forgiven…rescued…loved. Transformation is a process—a process requiring a sincere moment to face the consequences of our sin before the only One who can help us change. Through this interaction, Jesus gives us the power to change who we are. That's the focus for this week—the invitation to forgiveness and restoration that only comes as we bring our honest and open hearts to Jesus.

Time to take a deep breath. This is going to be a good week.

Day 1

Read John 8:1–11 (NASB). As you read, underline any names in green. Use yellow to highlight any words that God impresses upon your heart.

But Jesus went to the Mount of Olives. And early in the morning He came again into the temple area, and all the people were coming to Him; and He sat down and began teaching them. Now the scribes and the Pharisees brought a woman caught in the act of adultery, and after placing her in the center of the courtyard, they said to Him, "Teacher, this woman has been caught in the very act of committing adultery. Now in the Law, Moses commanded us to stone such women; what then do You say?" Now they were saying this to test Him, so that they might have grounds for accusing Him. But Jesus stooped down and with His finger wrote on the ground. When they persisted in asking Him, He straightened up and said to them, "He who is without sin among you, let him be the first to throw a stone at her." And again He stooped down and wrote on the ground. Now when they heard this, they began leaving, one by one, beginning with the older ones, and He was left alone, and the woman where she was, in the center of the courtyard. And straightening up, Jesus said to her, "Woman, where are they? Did no one condemn you?" She said, "No one, Lord." And Jesus said, "I do not condemn you, either. Go. From now on do not sin any longer."

Use this space to write down any insights God gave you while reading through the passage.

I was originally going to title this chapter, "Unnamed." But as I mentioned before, this woman already has a name by which the world knows her:

"A woman who had been caught in adultery."

When you study this portion of Scripture, you will discover that all the scholars refer to her in this way. If I had titled this chapter by her well-known name, you would likely have remembered the story before even reading it. Nowhere in all of my studying did I find her called by another name. Instead, she is a woman who is only identified by her sin.

Have you ever been identified by your sin? For some of us, maybe that is a reality. We are known by the mistakes we have made. For others, that identity may not be what others call us, rather we place that sinful identity on ourselves.

Liar. Thief. Failure.

Have there been times in your life when your struggle has become part of your identity? Regardless of whether that was because of your own choices or the choices of others, sometimes those names can become part of us. Take a minute to name some things you have carried with you as part of your own identity.

____

____

____

____

So often, we can even label ourselves with the things we carry. For me, it was a little more complicated.

My own story has been affected by adultery—in a different way than what this woman experienced, but affected nonetheless. My first marriage failed because of adultery, and the identity I carried because of that affected me for such a long time. When my husband walked out the door and into the arms of another woman...repeatedly...the enemy started to create my identity from the pieces that were left behind.

Divorced. Single mom. Rejected. Alone.

I think regardless of how we get these labels—whether it is our own fault or someone else's—one thing becomes increasingly clear. They are a result of sin.

Sin has a way of sticking with us. It can become part of us. It stains us.

I remember a time when my two oldest daughters were very little—young enough that both of them could fit inside the same stroller. I was in a place where I was trying to get my life back together, and in that process, I found myself with very little money. A church I had been a part of several years before was holding a rummage sale. Needing some clothes for the kids, I decided to go. Getting the girls out of the car and into the stroller, I walked from the parking lot up to the doors of the church. Because there were only steps, I had to push my stroller up a hill in order to get to the doors of the church. As I did, the wheels of the stroller slipped, and I slid face-first down into the mud that I didn't realize was there. The stroller flipped upside down, the girls landing in the mud with me. My white shirt was covered, my face was covered, and my children were covered in thick brown mud that refused to come clean with the homemade baby wipes I had with me. As much as I would have liked to go home that day, I still needed baby clothes. After doing the best I could to clean ourselves up, I carefully pulled the stroller up the stairs instead of trying the hill again. Ashamed, I walked through the doors to the church only to realize that there were door greeters who were still standing there. The same ones who watched me fall. The same ones that refused to offer any help to a struggling young mother. The same ones that took what little money I had left, as they commented on the terrible dirt on my shirt, eyeing the mud on our faces.

Years later, I realize there was so much more going on that day. I think in some ways, that situation was a parallel to what I experienced from the "church" in some of my darkest days. After my husband left, I wore the the stain of failure like a garment. People could see it. Not only could they see it, but they would comment on it—tell me that I should "repent" and maybe my husband would come back. They watched from the front doors of their churches, but never offered to help me up out of the mud. In fact, as we would start to clean ourselves up a bit, they would remind us that we were still dirty.

In kindergarten, a classmate told my daughter that I was going to hell because I was divorced.

As I got my follow-up HIV test, the "Christian" nurse commented on my assumed promiscuity.

The one time I was brave enough to try to go back to church, the Sunday school teacher questioned me on why I even bothered to come.

Do you hear what I am getting at? Regardless of my attempts to clean myself up from the stain of sin—not even my own sin but someone else's sin—the stain was still there.

That's the thing about a stain. It doesn't go away. It ruins the garment. It changes it. It's no longer valuable. It becomes known by the stain.

What things have stained you? Are there things you still carry? I know this is a rough way to start Day 1. But Sis, if this is about healing, we have to name the stain. We have to name it, so we can deal with it. And believe me, Jesus already knows. He. Already. Knows. Take a little time to name some things that you have carried with you, allowing them to stain those parts of your heart that carry an identity tainted by sin.

____

____

____

____

In the days to come, we will deal with our own sin. I am not negating personal responsibility, regardless of whether it's a lifestyle of sin or giving in to a temptation. But that's not today's focus.

Today? Today it's about her name: the woman caught in adultery. As we look at her through the perspective of Jesus, we see her called something else.

What does Jesus call her in verse 10? ____________________________________

When Jesus addresses her, He simply calls her "Woman."

If you never thought about that before, I want you to realize why this is significant. We remember from the study of Mary in Chapter 1, that the Western understanding of the name "woman" has a different connotation than what the culture in Jesus' time would have understood the word to mean. "Woman" was a term of endearment. It was the name He called His mother, and it's the name we are going to use for our study this week.

Woman.

Not a woman who had been caught in adultery.

Just...Woman.

You see, the world will try to define us by the struggle we carry.

Addicted. Unemployed. Imposter.

But Jesus? He gives us a new name. Even as He stands up for us, covering our sin, He calls us to Himself in the same term of affection that He used towards His mother. Do you know what that means?

Your struggle doesn't define you.

Did you hear me? Your struggle doesn't define you.

Only Jesus does.

Remember that as we study together this week. Remember that when the world throws a label at you that you keep fighting hard to shake. Our interaction with Jesus is the very thing that will change our struggle, our sin, and our lives enough that we can be called a new name. Our new identity is because of Him.

It's not that Jesus doesn't know what we are up to. He isn't ignorant of the things we keep struggling with. In fact, that's the very reason He came—to forgive us, to cover us, to defend us, to love us. And that love? That's what causes us to change. As we respond to His love, the natural inclination of our hearts will gradually become different. Our identity will no longer be wrapped up in our past, but instead it will align with our future.

Jesus gives us a new name. What is it?

Dear One. Loved. Woman.

Day 2

Read John 8:1-11 (NASB). As you read, highlight any timing words (first, after, then, etc.) with purple. Use yellow to highlight any words that God impresses upon your heart.

But Jesus went to the Mount of Olives. And early in the morning He came again into the temple area, and all the people were coming to Him; and He sat down and began teaching them. Now the scribes and the Pharisees brought a woman caught in the act of adultery, and after placing her in the center of the courtyard, they said to Him, "Teacher, this woman has been caught in the very act of committing adultery. Now in the Law, Moses commanded us to stone such women; what then do You say?" Now they were saying this to test Him, so that they might have grounds for accusing Him. But Jesus stooped down and with His finger wrote on the ground. When they persisted in asking Him, He straightened up and said to them, "He who is without sin among you, let him be the first to throw a stone at her." And again He stooped down and wrote on the ground. Now when they heard this, they began leaving, one by one, beginning with the older ones, and He was left alone, and the woman where she was, in the center of the courtyard. And straightening up, Jesus said to her, "Woman, where are they? Did no one condemn you?" She said, "No one, Lord." And Jesus said, "I do not condemn you, either. Go. From now on do not sin any longer."

Use this space to write down any insights God gave you while reading through the passage.

She was caught red-handed. Imagine this scene with me, if you will. Jesus was back at the temple, where He was sitting down and teaching. Take a look at verse 20, and write down anything you notice about the location where He was teaching.

Jesus was in the treasury. Do you know what part of the temple that was in? The women's court. Scholars agree that this earlier situation with the Woman was also in the same location, which means it happened in one of the most public and accessible parts of the temple. That's why the Woman in our story was able to be in that part of the temple in the first place. I think there were likely a couple of reasons why the treasury was chosen as the setting for this event. First, we know that the scribes and Pharisees were trying to trick Jesus, and it's likely they desired as large a crowd as possible to witness Jesus falling into their trap.

Beyond that though, I think Jesus intended for the Woman's story to be seen by as many people as possible, but for entirely different reasons.

What was Jesus doing in the temple? (vs 2) ______________________________

Jesus wasn't preaching in the temple, He was teaching. There's a difference. We see the word *didaskō* used here, which is different than what you would expect.

Typically, the word you would hear used for someone who instructs in the temple is *kēryssō,* which means to preach and proclaim.

Didaskō means to increase the understanding of the student**.** The meaning here is that the student would assimilate the knowledge as part of himself. It is the difference between hearing and knowing. Didaskō is the term that is used when Scripture refers to how Jesus taught, which was different than how the religious leaders of the time taught.

Jesus wants you to get it. He sits down and stays with you until you do.

What do you think He was teaching? I have to believe that He stayed seated because of didaskō. He was waiting for them to get it. Forgiveness. Grace. Love. Obedience.

Do we teach that in the church? We may preach it, but do we *teach* it? Do we make sure people understand it?

I am not against preaching or proclaiming. But I am for teaching, understanding, and putting what we are taught into practice.

Scribes (*Grammateus*) were the ones who were supposed to be interpreting the law for the people, teaching them about God's desire for reconciliation. Instead, they opposed Jesus, the very one God purposed for reconciliation. While Jesus is teaching the people the way the scribes were supposed to be doing, they are busy dragging this woman into the scene, exposing her shame and sin to everyone present.

Let's think through this for a moment. This Woman was caught in the act—red-handed—without a doubt of her guilt. I just want to take a quick minute to look at the original text. In this phrase, the word "caught" is *katalambanō* from the words ***kata,*** meaning intensive, and *lambanō,* meaning to take.

She was intensively taken into adultery. Another definition is to be seized or quickly overtaken.

That sounds like a lot of sins. You can't get out. Sin takes over. You almost feel helpless. You know it's wrong, but you do it anyway.

For this particular sin, she couldn't have acted alone. Yet nowhere do we find mention of the man who participated in this sin. While the scribes and Pharisees are correct in their espousal of the law of Moses, they are only saying half of the law. They were referring to Leviticus 20:10. Go ahead and look that up, and write down what the punishment is supposed to be.

Where was the man? They were both supposed to be put to death. Beyond that, it's likely that in order to "catch her in the act," they had to have some knowledge of what was going on. Many scholars believe that they trapped her in order to use her as a pawn in their bigger trap of Jesus. Knowing the law, Jesus would be caught between the justice the law required and the grace which He had become known for. Their hope was that they could condemn Him, no matter what answer He gave.

Sometimes we are entrapped by our own sin, and sometimes others pull us into sin, but regardless, we have all felt some level of "being caught" in our own lives. Although I have never committed adultery, I have been caught red-handed before. Most of us have. And that feeling you get when you know you've been caught—it's like a punch in the stomach.

No one else can be to blame for the things we choose to participate in ourselves. Personal responsibility has to accompany our choices. We will look at guilt a little more tomorrow, but today I want for us to deal with the emotion that accompanies guilt.

Think back to a time when you were caught "red-handed." Take a minute to reflect on the way it made you feel. Whether the sin was something big or little, I imagine you felt similarly to the way I did. Try to put into words what that felt like.

Could you identify the emotion? If you struggled to put it into words, let me share what I felt:

Shame.

Rather than share my own words on shame, I want you to spend a little time seeing what Scripture says about shame. Take some time to write out these verses.

Isaiah 50:7

Psalm 34:4–5

Romans 10:11

Zephaniah 3:19 ____

____

____

Isaiah 1:18 ____

____

____

Do you see what Jesus wants us to get? There's hope. We don't have to stay stuck in our shame. We don't have to carry it with us like a stain that refuses to be washed away. Instead, He wants to take that shame away from us as we realize our desperate need for a Savior who can rescue us from the things that hold us captive.

And that's the reason Jesus comes, He sits down, and He teaches us.

He wants us to get it. Jesus becomes our shame and our guilt and our sin, so that we can be restored to right relationship with God.

Sis? Jesus isn't going anywhere. He is sitting down with us until we get it.

Day 3

Read John 8:1–11 (NASB). As you read, circle any numbers with orange. Use yellow to highlight any words that God impresses upon your heart.

But Jesus went to the Mount of Olives. And early in the morning He came again into the temple area, and all the people were coming to Him; and He sat down and began teaching them. Now the scribes and the Pharisees brought a woman caught in the act of adultery, and after placing her in the center of the courtyard, they said to Him, "Teacher, this woman has been caught in the very act of committing adultery. Now in the Law, Moses commanded us to stone such women; what then do You say?" Now they were saying this to test Him, so that they might have grounds for accusing Him. But Jesus stooped down and with His finger wrote on the ground. When they persisted in asking Him, He straightened up and said to them, "He who is without sin among you, let him be the first to throw a stone at her." And again He stooped down and wrote on the ground. Now when they heard this, they began leaving, one by one, beginning with the older ones, and He was left alone, and the woman where she was, in the center of the courtyard. And straightening up, Jesus said to her, "Woman, where are they? Did no one condemn you?" She said, "No one, Lord." And Jesus said, "I do not condemn you, either. Go. From now on do not sin any longer."

Use this space to write down any insights God gave you while reading through the passage.

Guilt.

We have all been there. In fact, you may wonder why I started with the emotion that accompanies guilt—shame—before we dealt with guilt itself. Well, in all honesty, I am not sure we would even want to deal with guilt if there wasn't the emotion of shame attached to it. Have you ever met someone who never feels guilty? Never realizes their own responsibility for their actions, never allows themselves to take the blame when they are wrong? Many times, people can do that because they have dulled their senses to the emotion of shame. I think shame is part of what drives us to our knees, forcing us not only to recognize our own guilt but to deal with it.

When I talk about guilt, I am not talking about *feeling* guilty. That feeling is what we talked about yesterday when we looked at shame. There is a difference between the two. When we look at guilt, we are looking at it in terms of *being* guilty—of our responsibility when our own actions fall short. As we look to the story of the Woman, her guilt was indisputable. She was caught in the act.

Just like ours. Our guilt is indisputable.

Before we go any further, I want to give you some space to sort some things out if you need to. You may have had some issues screaming in your mind since yesterday that you need to confess and work through. But I want you to dig a little deeper than that. You may have some things that are knocking quietly on the inside of your heart—those things that have been done in secret. The things you think no one else knows about. The things you have justified and explained away because someone else caused them or led you into them. Those things. Jesus wants to take the guilt and shame of those things and exchange them for forgiveness, restoration, and peace. But before we can receive that, we need to name our sins, confront them, and confess them. For a long time, I refused to even pray about some things that I felt were justified either because someone else drove me to do them or because I felt God would understand why I ended up there. Regardless of how or why we ended up where we did, we still have to understand our guilt before we stand before the only One who doesn't carry the same stains we do.

Go ahead and spend a little time getting those things front and center.

If you are like me, you have labeled some things on this page that you didn't even want to admit, and you are hoping no one else ever sees them. I get it, and right now I am giving you permission to rip this page out when we are done and burn it. In fact, I would encourage you do so. But right now we have to deal with our sins. Take a deep breath.

There is good news. We have a Savior who longs to take that guilt away from us. That guilt we all have is the very reason He came to rescue us. He knows we all will arrive in this place—this place of condemnation and accusation.

We see Jesus, teaching in the temple, when this woman is brought before Him. As the men start to accuse her, baring her guilt for everyone to see, Jesus quietly responds. Just because He initially doesn't say anything, don't think for one second that He isn't responding.

What do we see Jesus do in response to the questioning of the scribes and Pharisees? (vs 6)

So many times, I have wondered what that meant. I think most of the times I have read that, I just assumed Jesus was playing in the dirt, thinking through a response to them. After studying this though, I have a different opinion.

They were in the temple, and the floor of the temple was paved with stones. So when Jesus reached down to write in the dirt, what He was writing would have been visible. In fact, the word for "wrote" in this verse is the word *graphō*. That word doesn't mean just doodling. It means to put something into writing or engraving. It refers to literal words on a parchment or paper.

How do the accusers respond to Jesus writing in the dirt? My sense is that they are so wrapped up with their agenda that they can't see His.

We are like that sometimes, aren't we? As believers? As the church? We get so wrapped up in our own agendas, our own demand for answers, that we can't see what Jesus is even doing.

They probably don't notice what He has written, and they keep questioning Him. What was His response? Go ahead and write it here. (vs 7–8)

Although I had a vague understanding of what a stoning would be like, I didn't really understand the gravity of what they were demanding.

In a traditional Jewish stoning, a punishment used for many types of communal sins, the guilty person would first be stripped naked. Then, they would be taken to a place outside of the city and thrown from a ledge at least twice as high as their own height. The witness to the crime would be the one to push them from the ledge. If the guilty person did not die from the fall alone, then the witness would take a large stone, throw it down, aiming at the person's chest. If that did not kill them, then the other witnesses would also take stones, throwing them down until the person died.

This. This is what she was facing. This is what they were asking Jesus about. This punishment, a humane way to kill someone in their eyes because it was quick, was the punishment they were asking Jesus to condemn her to. Jesus—a man known for His love and grace and mercy and compassion. Yet this is what the law required. Do you understand now the heaviness of His response? The trap they were trying to ensnare Him in?

Jesus responds by asking for the first stone to be cast, but only by whomever is without guilt. And what happens next changes things. What does Jesus do next?

____

As He bends back down to continue writing, their perspective begins to shift. Verse 9 says the accusers finally "heard it."

Heard, in the original text, is the word *akoúō,* which means to understand or comprehend. And after understanding what He was saying and doing, they were *elégchō*—shown to be wrong.

Do you realize this is the only account we have of Jesus writing something? After seeing their reaction, coupled with the fact that this is the only time we ever read of Jesus writing anything down, I don't think He was just doodling.

Then what was He writing? Most scholars think He was writing out a list of the sins of the witnesses, one by one.

The only One who was without sin…exposing the sin of the accusers.

Do you know who Scripture also refers to as the accuser?

Revelation 12:10______________________________________

Zechariah 3:1–2______________________________________

Ultimately, it was the enemy who was accusing her—who accuses us.

They were also attempting to accuse Jesus. But in the face of Jesus, the only One who is holy and set apart from the stains of sin, their own sin is revealed. You see, sin is revealed in the presence of a holy God. There is no way it can stay hidden. Our sin separates us from God, so by the very nature of *who He is*, sin cannot stay hidden. Jesus reveals, not only to them but to us, the very reasons why we have no authority to accuse anyone else.

We ourselves are guilty. We ourselves have sin that separates us from God. These men realized that one by one, as their own sin was revealed in Jesus' presence.

They were not qualified to condemn her because they themselves were guilty.

I want you to look up James 2:10 and write it here.

These men might not have been guilty of adultery; we may not be guilty of adultery. But we are still guilty. We are born with a sin nature, and there's no getting around it. We can either stand on the sidelines, calling out others for their sin, or we can walk them toward Jesus to find the forgiveness and grace that we ourselves have experienced.

Which path will you choose? When we realize our own need for a Savior, the sense that "our" sins are not as bad as "their" sins is taken away.

We are all guilty. And we all need Jesus.

Need a minute? I do. Take some time to pray, making sure your heart is clear.

Day 4

Read John 8:1–11 (NASB). As you read, underline divine acts of God, moves of the Holy Spirit, or anything supernatural with blue. Use yellow to highlight any words that God impresses upon your heart.

But Jesus went to the Mount of Olives. And early in the morning He came again into the temple area, and all the people were coming to Him; and He sat down and began teaching them. Now the scribes and the Pharisees brought a woman caught in the act of adultery, and after placing her in the center of the courtyard, they said to Him, "Teacher, this woman has been caught in the very act of committing adultery. Now in the Law, Moses commanded us to stone such women; what then do You say?" Now they were saying this to test Him, so that they might have grounds for accusing Him. But Jesus stooped down and with His finger wrote on the ground. When they persisted in asking Him, He straightened up and said to them, "He who is without sin among you, let him be the first to throw a stone at her." And again He stooped down and wrote on the ground. Now when they heard this, they began leaving, one by one, beginning with the older ones, and He was left alone, and the woman where she was, in the center of the courtyard. And straightening up, Jesus said to her, "Woman, where are they? Did no one condemn you?" She said, "No one, Lord." And Jesus said, "I do not condemn you, either. Go. From now on do not sin any longer."

Use this space to write down any insights God gave you while reading through the passage.

As I shared earlier this week, I experienced a season in my life where I walked in shame, carrying with me such a heaviness that I felt like a dark heavy blanket was laid across my shoulders. Regardless of how I got there, that's where I was for a very long time. One of the hardest things about that season was the loneliness. It wasn't that I didn't try to get out of that place, but my attempts were just met with more pain. No one wanted the divorced, single mom at their mommy group. Or even more hurtful, at their church small group. I was treated almost as if my situation were contagious. Or maybe they weren't prepared for brokenness. Either way, that season left me with some scars. The hard part, more than a decade later, is seeing some of those same people go through their own hard seasons. It's hard because I know how they feel. But now? Now they don't back away when they see me. They welcome the smile, the helping hand, the hug, the prayer. Now they know what I was going through, and they themselves need what I was desperate for.

One of the things I have learned is that there are seasons in life—seasons of pain, joy, sorrow, and even seasons of sin—before we come into obedience and conviction of the Holy Spirit. It's part of the human experience. What I think the scribes and the Pharisees in our story failed to realize was that their current season didn't nullify their previous ones.

Jesus makes a statement to them, then bends down to write in the dirt again. This second time illicits a different response than the first. What happens this time? (vs 9)

The original text refers to this concept with the word *suneídēsis* which refers to one's own conscience coming forward as a witness. In short, it's self-awareness.

To me, this indicates that the words Jesus wrote meant something to them personally. While we can't say for certain what He wrote in the dirt, I think it goes back to what we studied earlier this week. Jesus sits and stays with us until we "get" the message He is trying to teach. And in this situation, I believe He is trying to teach them about mercy, forgiveness, and grace.

One by one, starting with the oldest in the group and working down to the youngest, the accusers disappear. Perhaps the oldest were the wisest—the elders were able to grasp more quickly the connection Jesus was making. Or perhaps their list of sins was longer. Regardless, they slip away. The accusers have become the accused, and they realize they are just as guilty as the Woman.

None were left who were qualified to cast the first stone. None but Jesus.

The reality is, these men likely could have been guilty of something that they should have faced consequences for themselves. Maybe the way in which they treated the Woman. Maybe other things that they kept hidden. But either way, Jesus' wisdom in handling this situation shows us something about how we need to handle people who come to us still stuck in their brokenness and mess.

Mercy, forgiveness, grace.

Yes, we need to guide them towards repentance. Or healing. Or whatever else Jesus wants to do with them. But casting a stone? That's not our role. Jesus will handle addressing their sin. Our role is just to get them there. If we respond with grace and mercy when we meet broken people, it changes things. The way we speak to them, the way we help them, the way we love them allows others the opportunity to come closer to Jesus, as they see Him in us.

You see, the reason Jesus was so radical in His time was because of His love. He dared to love those that others rejected. His love drew people in. It's still that way, yet as we represent Him to a lost and broken world, I think we sometimes forget that. We forget we are to love people the way He did—the way He does. Do they need to change? I'm sure. Do they need to deal with their own sin? Of course. Are there things they are doing that you know are wrong—that they know are wrong? Yep. But how can we ever expect them to get to Jesus if we send them away before they get the chance?

Take a few minutes to write out what Scripture says about how and why we are to love each other.

John 13:34 ____

____

____

Mark 12:31 ____

____

____

1 John 4:19 ____

____

____

Romans 13:8 ______________________________

____

____

Matthew 22:37–39 ______________________________

____

____

I'm sure you could add even more Scriptures about love that are familiar to you. What these verses teach us is that the Christian life is supposed to represent the love of Christ, regardless of the behavior of the people we are called to love. People "behaving" shouldn't make us love or accept them more. In fact, the people who have the most mess and sin in their lives are the very ones we are called to point toward Christ. We can't expect non-believers to act as believers do—and even believers find themselves in a mess sometimes. I know I have.

I want you to take a little time to think through two aspects of self-awareness that we touched on today.

What times in your life have you needed the love and grace of other believers?

____

____

____

Did you get what you needed? ______________________________

____

____

How did their behavior impact your situation? ______________________________

____

____

How would your experience have changed if the believers in your life had acted differently? Maybe no believers were around you at that time. How would things have been different if there were?

If you had a relationship with a believer or group of believers who helped you walk toward Jesus, I am so thankful for that. If you didn't, I am so incredibly sorry. I think the key, regardless of what you experienced, is to recognize the power wrapped up in the role of loving people and pointing them to Jesus when they need it most.

Now let's take this one step further. It's time for our own suneídēsis to affect us in such a way that we live differently.

Is there someone in your life who you have been quick to accuse, condemn, or judge?

How might your present attitude toward them affect them? Not just today, but for eternity?

Is that action or behavior what you would need if you were in a similar situation? If not, what *would* you need?

Take a little time to see if the Lord reveals someone He is calling you to reach out to in love. Maybe you need to go back to someone who you responded to poorly before. Either way, allow the Lord to work here in this space.

Maybe you think it's too late to repair the damage because of the way you treated the person in the past. Sis, it's never too late. We need each other. Realize that you have your own things written in the dirt.

My prayer is that we will start to see our sisters—our lost and hurting, stuck in their mess sisters—and help them find their way out. Will you join me in that? Praying for you.

Day 5

Read John 8:1–11 (NASB). As you read, underline all the verbs, the action words, in pink. Use yellow to highlight any words that God impresses upon your heart.

But Jesus went to the Mount of Olives. And early in the morning He came again into the temple area, and all the people were coming to Him; and He sat down and began teaching them. Now the scribes and the Pharisees brought a woman caught in the act of adultery, and after placing her in the center of the courtyard, they said to Him, "Teacher, this woman has been caught in the very act of committing adultery. Now in the Law, Moses commanded us to stone such women; what then do You say?" Now they were saying this to test Him, so that they might have grounds for accusing Him. But Jesus stooped down and with His finger wrote on the ground. When they persisted in asking Him, He straightened up and said to them, "He who is without sin among you, let him be the first to throw a stone at her." And again He stooped down and wrote on the ground. Now when they heard this, they began leaving, one by one, beginning with the older ones, and He was left alone, and the woman where she was, in the center of the courtyard. And straightening up, Jesus said to her, "Woman, where are they? Did no one condemn you?" She said, "No one, Lord." And Jesus said, "I do not condemn you, either. Go. From now on do not sin any longer."

Use this space to write down any insights God gave you while reading through the passage.

Sin.

We have been talking about it all week. Today we have to deal with it. We looked at the ways in which Jesus responded in grace this week, but we can't stop there. Jesus doesn't stop there.

One of the common arguments over this portion of Scripture—what they would have liked to trap Jesus with—is that Jesus broke the law by allowing her to go free. At first, I think I probably had a similar thought.

But Sis, this is really important, and I want to make sure you get it. Jesus kept the law; it wasn't possible for Him to break the law because of who He was. He kept the law by taking her place. Sentenced to die, He took her place. What are the last words Jesus says to her? (vs 11)

Do you know what condemnation means? It means to hand down a judgement. By leading her toward the path of forgiveness, He was also heading down the path of being condemned in her place. That decision wasn't without cost. It's just that she was worth the cost to Him. And so are you.

While Jesus offers forgiveness and grace, He also gives the command to change. In order to stay in close relationship with Him, the very nature of that relationship demanded it.

How was it that He was able to let her go free? The same way He lets us go free. It's not that He didn't call adultery a sin. He did. But instead of condemnation…a sentence of death which she deserved for her sin…instead, He extended grace.

The sin of the men excluded them from condemning her, and Jesus is the only One without sin—the only One qualified to throw a stone at her. Instead? He releases her into repentance.

Write 2 Corinthians 5:21 in the space below.

He became the very sin that held her captive, so she could experience true freedom. I want you to see something that struck me as I was reading this week.

What do the scribes and Pharisees call Jesus? ______________________________

What does the Woman call Jesus?______________________________

What's the difference here? The men called Him the Master or the teacher. She called Him Lord. By calling Him Lord, she was recognizing who He was…her Savior.

That's love. That's forgiveness. That's freedom. And that's restoration.

Throughout our time together this week, we saw Jesus walk the tension between justice and grace.

The woman knew she was guilty. She knew she deserved death. They both did. Yet Jesus offers her something so valuable, so precious that it transforms her. You see, Sis, it's grace that transforms us.

Our obedience comes as a result of a relationship with Jesus, and the relationship comes when we realize what grace is. Grace is what leads us to respond to the invitation of Jesus. When we realize the guilt of our sin, we come to understand the true meaning of grace.

I want you to write out some key verses that teach us about this transformative aspect. Feel free to use different versions of Scripture. Sometimes that's helpful when we are trying to dig a little deeper into what Jesus is trying to teach us.

2 Timothy 1:9 ______________________________

____

____

Ephesians 4:7 ______________________________

____

____

John 1:14 ______________________________

____

____

Ephesians 1:7

Colossians 1:6

Acts 20:24

2 Corinthians 12:9

Do you get it, Sis? Grace is God's love for us. Grace is what Jesus offers to us. Grace is what changes us, if we let it. When we truly understand the gift of grace Jesus offers to us despite our sin—in fact, because of it—we are met with a decision. We can choose to walk away, or we can choose to hear.

And the Woman who Jesus met at the temple? When Jesus offers her grace, *she hears.* Praying the same for you, Sis.

During the rest of the time we have together today, I want to encourage you to spend some time just receiving the grace that Jesus is offering.

CHAPTER FOUR

Martha

A Woman of Assertiveness • John 11:1–44 (NASB)

This week, we are starting the first part of a larger two-week study on two sisters: Martha and Mary, two of my favorite women in the New Testament. You will notice this passage is a little longer than we have had in the past couple of weeks, but I am hoping by now you are starting to get the hang of the color method of study. The longer passages help us to understand a little better the value in studying the Scriptures in this way.

Many details about Martha and Mary are intertwined each time we see them in Scripture, so it is hard to separate them when we study. However, to approach their unique relationships with Jesus, I am attempting to do that very thing. Their stories will inevitably overlap, but I believe we will find some important lessons to learn here with regard to how we interact as sisters, as believers, and as different personalities. We will take extra time to look at each woman individually; however, there will be moments when we will consider the greater context, which is found in their relationship to each other. Sound good? Then let's get started.

Day 1

Read John 11:1–44 (NASB). As you read, underline any names in green. Use yellow to highlight any words that God impresses upon your heart.

Now a certain man was sick: Lazarus of Bethany, the village of Mary and her sister Martha. And it was the Mary who anointed the Lord with ointment, and wiped His feet with her hair, whose brother Lazarus was sick. So the sisters sent word to Him, saying, "Lord, behold, he whom You love is sick." But when Jesus heard this, He said, "This sickness is not meant for death, but is for the glory of God, so that the Son of God may be glorified by it." (Now Jesus loved Martha and her sister, and Lazarus.) So when He heard that he was sick, He then stayed two days longer in the place where He was. Then after this He said to the disciples, "Let's go to Judea again." The disciples said to Him, "Rabbi, the Jews were just now seeking to stone You, and yet You are going there again?" Jesus replied, "Are there not twelve hours in the day? If anyone walks during the day, he does not stumble, because he sees the light of this world. But if anyone walks during the night, he stumbles, because the light is not in him." This He said, and after this He said to them, "Our friend Lazarus has fallen asleep; but I am going so that I may awaken him from sleep." The disciples then said to Him, "Lord, if he has fallen asleep, he will come out of it." Now Jesus had spoken of his death, but they thought that He was speaking about actual sleep. So Jesus then said to them plainly, "Lazarus died, and I am glad for your sakes that I was not there, so that you may believe; but let's go to him." Therefore Thomas, who was called Didymus, said to his fellow disciples, "Let's also go, so that we may die with Him!" So when Jesus came, He found that he had already been in the tomb four days. Now Bethany was near Jerusalem, about fifteen stadia away; and many of the Jews had come to Martha and Mary, to console them about their brother. So then Martha, when she heard that Jesus was coming, went to meet Him, but Mary stayed in the house. Martha then said to Jesus, "Lord, if You had been here, my brother would not have died. Even now I know that whatever You ask of God, God will give You." Jesus said to her,

"Your brother will rise from the dead." Martha said to Him, "I know that he will rise in the resurrection on the last day." Jesus said to her, "I am the resurrection and the life; the one who believes in Me will live, even if he dies, and everyone who lives and believes in Me will never die. Do you believe this?" She said to Him, "Yes, Lord; I have come to believe that You are the Christ, the Son of God, and He who comes into the world." When she had said this, she left and called Mary her sister, saying secretly, "The Teacher is here and is calling for you." And when she heard this, she got up quickly and came to Him. Now Jesus had not yet come into the village, but was still in the place where Martha met Him. Then the Jews who were with her in the house and were consoling her, when they saw that Mary had gotten up quickly and left, they followed her, thinking that she was going to the tomb to weep there. So when Mary came to the place where Jesus was, she saw Him and fell at His feet, saying to Him, "Lord, if You had been here, my brother would not have died." Therefore when Jesus saw her weeping, and the Jews who came with her also weeping, He was deeply moved in spirit and was troubled, and He said, "Where have you laid him?" They said to Him, "Lord, come and see." Jesus wept. So the Jews were saying, "See how He loved him!" But some of them said, "Could this man, who opened the eyes of the man who was blind, not have also kept this man from dying?" So Jesus, again being deeply moved within, came to the tomb. Now it was a cave, and a stone was lying against it. Jesus said, "Remove the stone." Martha, the sister of the deceased, said to Him, "Lord, by this time there will be a stench, for he has been dead four days." Jesus said to her, "Did I not say to you that if you believe, you will see the glory of God?" So they removed the stone. Then Jesus raised His eyes, and said, "Father, I thank You that You have heard Me. But I knew that You always hear Me; nevertheless, because of the people standing around I said it, so that they may believe that You sent Me." And when He had said these things, He cried out with a loud voice, "Lazarus, come forth." Out came the man who had died, bound hand and foot with wrappings, and his face was wrapped around with a cloth. Jesus said to them, "Unbind him, and let him go."

Use this space to write down any insights God gave you while reading through the passage.

I must admit, Martha's story has been one of the more difficult for me to write. Why? Because I am a Martha. If you have heard Martha and Mary's story taught in church, like so many of us, you may already have a sense of which sister you are more like. But again, as we did in our previous weeks, we are going to start from scratch and assume we know nothing about these two. We are going to back up a bit and take a look at the first time we see these sisters in Scripture. I think that will give you a point of reference that explains the dynamic and difference between Martha and Mary. Let's take a few moments to read through the story of the sisters in Luke 10:38-42 (NASB).

> *Now as they were traveling along, He entered a village; and a woman named Martha welcomed Him into her home. And she had a sister called Mary, who was also seated at the Lord's feet, and was listening to His word. But Martha was distracted with all her preparations; and she came up to Him and said, "Lord, do You not care that my sister has left me to do the serving by myself? Then tell her to help me." But the Lord answered and said to her, "Martha, Martha, you are worried and distracted by many things; but only one thing is necessary; for Mary has chosen the good part, which shall not be taken away from her.*

Well, there it is. Initial thoughts? Mine are something like: Martha, Martha, Martha.... (Picture me slowly shaking my head).

The thing is, I think poor Martha gets a bad rap here. Most people don't dig a little deeper into her story. They just come down on her and think she should loosen up. If I am honest, there have been times in my life when I have been more of a Martha than a Mary. Well, most of the time. It's not that I don't *want* to be a Mary. It's just that I have too much stuff to do. Ever been there?

Let's just take a look at some of the initial characteristics of Martha that we find in this short list:

Independent
Runs her mouth
Impulsive
Hard worker
Doesn't mind complaining to Jesus

Yep…. That's me. I love Jesus. But I also love getting stuff done. Especially when these people are all my responsibility. If I am honest, when I read this first story, I was hoping Jesus would tell Mary to get to work. I know, I'm terrible…but I'm honest! He doesn't though. Instead, Jesus calls Martha to Himself.

I think back over moments I have had in my own life when I have been experiencing burn out, feeling like I am the only one who is doing all the work—in ministry, as a mom, as a wife. Martha's words, even if I don't say them out loud, certainly have gone through my mind.

Scholars believe that Martha owned her own home. In Martha's time, welcoming a rabbi into your home was kind of a big deal. The Jewish culture placed a very high value on the study of the Scriptures. Teachers of the law would travel from town to town teaching, asking for no pay in return. Their compensation came in the form of food and shelter. Hospitality of the host was not only expected socially, but religiously. Most likely, Martha thought her work preparing the meal for Jesus and the others was virtuous. When she encouraged Mary to join her, it's also possible that her intention was good—that she felt this was the way they were supposed to serve when having Jesus in her home.

We can tell from her words, though, that trouble is brewing just under the surface. Her frustration with serving spills out when she voices her complaint to Jesus.

Martha is so busy doing the work preparing for the ministry of Jesus that she couldn't, or wouldn't, take the time to allow Jesus to minister to her.

Well, that stings a little.

Then again, every time I complain to Jesus in a similar way, He has a similar response.

"Come here."

What does Jesus say in verse 42? ______________________________

____

There's only one thing necessary. In fact, He calls it the "good part."

The one thing that was necessary is still the "good part" of serving: connection with Jesus. Joining Him in what He is doing. Our service to Him *has* to start here, or a lack of connection will be reflected in our words, our hearts, and our attitudes. If you find Martha's side of the story resonating with you, perhaps it's time to sit down at the feet of Jesus.

I don't know if you are like me, but my temptation is to think, "Well, sure. But the work still needs to be done."

I get that. But can I let you in on a little secret? Someone else who has already sat at the feet of Jesus will do the work. Or they won't. Maybe it won't get done at all. But that's not your primary concern. Your primary concern is your relationship with Jesus.

If we can get this concept, then we are freed from the burden of serving Him. Serving should be the natural overflow of our hearts in response to being with Jesus. Instead, so many times we allow the serving part to overtake the relationship part.

That's not what Jesus asks of us, despite what anyone else asks of us. If you are in full-time ministry, if you are serving as a lay person, or even if you are serving in your own home, there is only one thing Jesus asks of us.

"Come here."

Listen to me, Sis. I need you to understand this one thing before we move on from this part of Martha's story. Martha is loved for who she *is*, not for what she *does*.

Same goes for you. You don't have to earn His love. You already have it. You always did.

Day 2

Read John 11:1–44 (NASB). As you read, highlight any timing words (first, after, then, etc.) with purple. Use yellow to highlight any words that God impresses upon your heart.

Now a certain man was sick: Lazarus of Bethany, the village of Mary and her sister Martha. And it was the Mary who anointed the Lord with ointment, and wiped His feet with her hair, whose brother Lazarus was sick. So the sisters sent word to Him, saying, "Lord, behold, he whom You love is sick." But when Jesus heard this, He said, "This sickness is not meant for death, but is for the glory of God, so that the Son of God may be glorified by it." (Now Jesus loved Martha and her sister, and Lazarus.) So when He heard that he was sick, He then stayed two days longer in the place where He was. Then after this He said to the disciples, "Let's go to Judea again." The disciples said to Him, "Rabbi, the Jews were just now seeking to stone You, and yet You are going there again?" Jesus replied, "Are there not twelve hours in the day? If anyone walks during the day, he does not stumble, because he sees the light of this world. But if anyone walks during the night, he stumbles, because the light is not in him." This He said, and after this He said to them, "Our friend Lazarus has fallen asleep; but I am going so that I may awaken him from sleep." The disciples then said to Him, "Lord, if he has fallen asleep, he will come out of it." Now Jesus had spoken of his death, but they thought that He was speaking about actual sleep. So Jesus then said to them plainly, "Lazarus died, and I am glad for your sakes that I was not there, so that you may believe; but let's go to him." Therefore Thomas, who was called Didymus, said to his fellow disciples, "Let's also go, so that we may die with Him!" So when Jesus came, He found that he had already been in the tomb four days. Now Bethany was near Jerusalem, about fifteen stadia away; and many of the Jews had come to Martha and Mary, to console them about their brother. So then Martha, when she heard that Jesus was coming, went to meet Him, but Mary stayed in the house. Martha then said to Jesus, "Lord, if You had been here, my brother would not have died. Even now I know that whatever You ask of God, God will give You." Jesus

said to her, "Your brother will rise from the dead." Martha said to Him, "I know that he will rise in the resurrection on the last day." Jesus said to her, "I am the resurrection and the life; the one who believes in Me will live, even if he dies, and everyone who lives and believes in Me will never die. Do you believe this?" She said to Him, "Yes, Lord; I have come to believe that You are the Christ, the Son of God, and He who comes into the world." When she had said this, she left and called Mary her sister, saying secretly, "The Teacher is here and is calling for you." And when she heard this, she got up quickly and came to Him. Now Jesus had not yet come into the village, but was still in the place where Martha met Him. Then the Jews who were with her in the house and were consoling her, when they saw that Mary had gotten up quickly and left, they followed her, thinking that she was going to the tomb to weep there. So when Mary came to the place where Jesus was, she saw Him and fell at His feet, saying to Him, "Lord, if You had been here, my brother would not have died." Therefore when Jesus saw her weeping, and the Jews who came with her also weeping, He was deeply moved in spirit and was troubled, and He said, "Where have you laid him?" They said to Him, "Lord, come and see." Jesus wept. So the Jews were saying, "See how He loved him!" But some of them said, "Could this man, who opened the eyes of the man who was blind, not have also kept this man from dying?" So Jesus, again being deeply moved within, came to the tomb. Now it was a cave, and a stone was lying against it. Jesus said, "Remove the stone." Martha, the sister of the deceased, said to Him, "Lord, by this time there will be a stench, for he has been dead four days." Jesus said to her, "Did I not say to you that if you believe, you will see the glory of God?" So they removed the stone. Then Jesus raised His eyes, and said, "Father, I thank You that You have heard Me. But I knew that You always hear Me; nevertheless, because of the people standing around I said it, so that they may believe that You sent Me." And when He had said these things, He cried out with a loud voice, "Lazarus, come forth." Out came the man who had died, bound hand and foot with wrappings, and his face was wrapped around with a cloth. Jesus said to them, "Unbind him, and let him go."

Use this space to write down any insights God gave you while reading through the passage.

Yesterday we spent time studying another part of Scripture, and I hope you understand now why we did that. Today we are going to get into the main part of our study by looking at the story of Lazarus.

Picking up where we left off, I want to remind you that Martha is loved for who she *is*, not for what she *does*. Now, let's take a closer look at the kind of relationship Jesus had with this family.

As you may have noticed, the home of these siblings is a place where Jesus spent some time. In addition to that, later on in the biblical timeline, the triumphal entry will start very close to their home, and Jesus will also ascend nearby. I think it's significant that the home of Martha is central to the gospel story.

Martha's home was located in a village called Bethany. In the original text, Bethany was the name *Beit-Anyah,* or house of poverty. Biblical Bethany was a center to care for poor and sick people. Does that hit you the way it hits me? The place where Jesus spent a lot of time. The place where Jesus decided to perform His last miracle before His death. The place that would change the way people felt about Him and recognized Him. The place where His glory would be shown in a powerful way. That place was where the poor and sick people were.

Miracles happen where the poor and sick are. I've seen it first hand. I don't know why that fact surprised me the way it did, but it makes me love Jesus even more.

In the Bible story, we are introduced to Lazarus in terms of the relationship between Martha and Mary. Because of this, we realize that Jesus' relationship with the sisters is likely the more prominent one. In addition, John refers to Mary as if the reader has already heard her story. There is an assumption of familiarity. I love that. I want that. I want people to recognize me, and my family, because of my relationship with Jesus.

Let's spend a little time looking at verse 5. Go ahead and write it here.

We know that this family is special in Jesus' eyes. Several times throughout this chapter, Scripture mentions that they were loved. We also see them referred to as loved by other people. But I want to draw your attention to verse 5, which explains *how* Jesus loved them.

In the Greek, there are actually four words that describe love. That's a foreign concept to us because we lump all types of love together into one word in the English language. Let's look at the differences.

Erao: This is the type of love described in the Book of Song of Solomon. I'm not gonna tell you to go there right now. If you haven't read that book before, make sure you're alone when you read it.

Storgeo: This type of love can be found in Romans 12:10. Go ahead and look it up and write it here.

Phileo: This type of love can be found in John 13:34–35. Take a few minutes to write that here.

Agapao: One of the best examples of this is found in John 3:16. Even if you don't have to look it up because you already know it, write it out here.

To review, here's a quick summary of what the four words mean:

Erao: Romantic, sexual love; the love between a husband and wife

Storgeo: Family unit love, describing the love between parents and children or siblings; or sometimes refers to a longer-term, social bond like "best friends"

Phileo: Friendship love and affection, often refers to how followers of Christ are recognized

Agapao: Godly love

Which word do you think is used for the love Jesus had for these siblings? Why do you think that?

____

____

____

____

Do you want to know the answer? It's agapao. Does that surprise you a little? It surprised me. I thought the word would have been phileo. In fact, the times that the love between Jesus and the siblings is mentioned by other people, phileo is used. But if you notice, those other times are all observations from the outside looking in. Only when John describes how Jesus felt towards them do we see agapao used.

Now, if you're like me, you may assume Jesus just felt that way about everyone. The very nature of who Jesus is leads us to make that assumption. And we're not wrong. However, the only other time agapao is specifically mentioned with regard to another person is when Jesus talks about the Beloved Disciple, who many scholars believe to be John himself.

I don't think it's an accident that agapao is used here. The word itself refers to the kind of love that is rooted in the mind and will. It's the kind of unselfish love someone shows when their action is done for the best outcome and benefit of the person being loved.

Think through that with me for a minute. Jesus loved Martha, Mary, and Lazarus in such a way that He would do what was best for them. We will spend some more time on this tomorrow, but for today, I want you to think through the facts.

Jesus was acting in a way that was in the best interest of Martha because of His love for her and her family. Jesus got word that Lazarus was sick. Jesus knew that by the time He got back to Bethany, Lazarus would already be dead. Still, He waited two more days.

Have you ever felt like you had something die while waiting on Jesus? Heavy, I know. But I want you to remember that God is for you, not against you. We are going to pick this apart a little more throughout the rest of the week. Right now though, I want you to write out the thing you are thinking about right now. Maybe a dream, a career, a ministry, or even someone you loved died. I don't know if you're like me, but this is hard to come to grips with. Some things in my life have died while I was waiting on Jesus. Yet I know He loves me and works in my best interest, even if I don't understand. Take a little time to work through that here. Praying for you, Sis, as you start to allow Jesus to heal this place that has been hidden in your heart. I'm with you.

Day 3

Read John 11:1-44 (NASB). As you read, circle any numbers with orange. Use yellow to highlight any words that God impresses upon your heart.

Now a certain man was sick: Lazarus of Bethany, the village of Mary and her sister Martha. And it was the Mary who anointed the Lord with ointment, and wiped His feet with her hair, whose brother Lazarus was sick. So the sisters sent word to Him, saying, "Lord, behold, he whom You love is sick." But when Jesus heard this, He said, "This sickness is not meant for death, but is for the glory of God, so that the Son of God may be glorified by it." (Now Jesus loved Martha and her sister, and Lazarus.) So when He heard that he was sick, He then stayed two days longer in the place where He was. Then after this He said to the disciples, "Let's go to Judea again." The disciples said to Him, "Rabbi, the Jews were just now seeking to stone You, and yet You are going there again?" Jesus replied, "Are there not twelve hours in the day? If anyone walks during the day, he does not stumble, because he sees the light of this world. But if anyone walks during the night, he stumbles, because the light is not in him." This He said, and after this He said to them, "Our friend Lazarus has fallen asleep; but I am going so that I may awaken him from sleep." The disciples then said to Him, "Lord, if he has fallen asleep, he will come out of it." Now Jesus had spoken of his death, but they thought that He was speaking about actual sleep. So Jesus then said to them plainly, "Lazarus died, and I am glad for your sakes that I was not there, so that you may believe; but let's go to him." Therefore Thomas, who was called Didymus, said to his fellow disciples, "Let's also go, so that we may die with Him!" So when Jesus came, He found that he had already been in the tomb four days. Now Bethany was near Jerusalem, about fifteen stadia away; and many of the Jews had come to Martha and Mary, to console them about their brother. So then Martha, when she heard that Jesus was coming, went to meet Him, but Mary stayed in the house. Martha then said to Jesus, "Lord, if You had been here, my brother would not have died. Even now I know that whatever You ask of God, God will give You." Jesus

said to her, "Your brother will rise from the dead." Martha said to Him, "I know that he will rise in the resurrection on the last day." Jesus said to her, "I am the resurrection and the life; the one who believes in Me will live, even if he dies, and everyone who lives and believes in Me will never die. Do you believe this?" She said to Him, "Yes, Lord; I have come to believe that You are the Christ, the Son of God, and He who comes into the world." When she had said this, she left and called Mary her sister, saying secretly, "The Teacher is here and is calling for you." And when she heard this, she got up quickly and came to Him. Now Jesus had not yet come into the village, but was still in the place where Martha met Him. Then the Jews who were with her in the house and were consoling her, when they saw that Mary had gotten up quickly and left, they followed her, thinking that she was going to the tomb to weep there. So when Mary came to the place where Jesus was, she saw Him and fell at His feet, saying to Him, "Lord, if You had been here, my brother would not have died." Therefore when Jesus saw her weeping, and the Jews who came with her also weeping, He was deeply moved in spirit and was troubled, and He said, "Where have you laid him?" They said to Him, "Lord, come and see." Jesus wept. So the Jews were saying, "See how He loved him!" But some of them said, "Could this man, who opened the eyes of the man who was blind, not have also kept this man from dying?" So Jesus, again being deeply moved within, came to the tomb. Now it was a cave, and a stone was lying against it. Jesus said, "Remove the stone." Martha, the sister of the deceased, said to Him, "Lord, by this time there will be a stench, for he has been dead four days." Jesus said to her, "Did I not say to you that if you believe, you will see the glory of God?" So they removed the stone. Then Jesus raised His eyes, and said, "Father, I thank You that You have heard Me. But I knew that You always hear Me; nevertheless, because of the people standing around I said it, so that they may believe that You sent Me." And when He had said these things, He cried out with a loud voice, "Lazarus, come forth." Out came the man who had died, bound hand and foot with wrappings, and his face was wrapped around with a cloth. Jesus said to them, "Unbind him, and let him go."

Use this space to write down any insights God gave you while reading through the passage.

Four days. I'm sure you picked up on that just now, especially since we're focusing on numbers today. Four long days Lazarus has been dead by the time Jesus gets back to Bethany. The reason? Verse 6.

Go ahead and write that here.

Remember, this verse is right after verse 5 where we learn that Jesus loved Martha with agapao kind of love—the love that does what's best for the person.

Does that confuse you at all? If Jesus loved them, why would He wait? Does that make sense to you? It didn't to me at first. Even less so when I considered how close He was. In verse 18 the Bible tells us how far away Jesus was from them when He got the news about Lazarus being ill.

How far away was He? (vs 18) ______________________________

Two miles. Two miles! Think about somewhere that's two miles away from your house. Now think about how long it would take to walk there. I guess when I think about it in those terms, I can start to understand why Martha responded the way she did.

How did Martha react when He finally arrived in Bethany? (vs 20–22). Write down anything you notice.

I notice a couple of things:

1. Martha left the house and went to meet Him. This may not seem like a big deal to you, but consider what this meant to her. In Jewish culture, there was a practice referred to as "sitting shivah." This meant that the first week after a close relative died, the family would mourn them sitting on the floor of their house. Other members of the family and community would bring food and other comforts. In fact, this is still practiced today in many traditional Jewish homes. By leaving the house, Martha broke with the cultural tradition, perhaps impulsively, to go out and meet Jesus. And when I say "meet," let's look at that objectively. What does verse 30 say about where she met up with Jesus?

He had not yet come into the village. We aren't exactly sure how far away that was, but it's not like He was right outside her front door. She had a minute. You can almost see her get more mad with each footstep. Once she reached Jesus, we discover the second thing I noticed.

2. Their relationship was strong enough that she could complain to Him. She isn't whining about her family's misfortune but speaking the truth as she perceives it. I actually find it to be a remarkable statement of her faith in Him, the way she boldly claims that if He had been there, Lazarus wouldn't have died. But even in her faith, she confronts Jesus about where He was in the midst of her circumstances.

Ever been there? Ever ranted to God about a promise He made and it felt like He didn't come through? I so have. More than once. Me in my self-righteous, indignant moments. I'm not proud. I told you this was a hard chapter for me to write, but I am being truthful in a way that I hope helps you to realize you're not alone. We all have those moments. You know what else? Jesus knew Martha was going to react this way, just like He knew Lazarus had died. He knew her and He still did what was best for her, even though He knew she wasn't going to like it.

So the question remains. Why did Jesus wait so long? Even if He knew He was going to resurrect Lazarus, why put Martha and Mary through the agony of grief for one second longer than He had to?

Jesus knew what was best for them…and not just for them, but for us.

Even now, there is a Jewish belief that after death, the soul does not leave the body right away. In fact, the Jews believe that the soul of someone hovers over the body for a period of three days. In some cases, they believed a resurrection might even be possible during that three day period. But by day four, decay starts to set in. Any hope of someone still being alive is gone by day four. Some would say day four is the day that hope is gone.

Do you get it now? Jesus waited until the fourth day so that His glory would be manifested in such a way that no one would doubt it. It was the timing that would allow the most people to come to faith in Him. And remember where they were—Bethany. The place for the poor, the vulnerable, the sick. They needed hope.

Martha knew how long it would take to get from where Jesus was to where Lazarus was. In her mind, He was too late. Maybe she even felt that if He got there within the first three days, He could have resurrected her brother. Even though we see her respond with words of faith, you have to wonder what was going on inside her heart.

I have to wonder, what's going on inside yours? Take a little time if you need it to process, pray, complain, whatever you need to do. I get it. And so does He.

Waiting on Jesus can seem offensive to us, but there was a reason.

Have you ever had the thought, "What's taking so long?" when waiting on Jesus for your miracle?

He loved them…. So He stayed where He was for two more days. Because Jesus loved them, He waited.

When this happens in my own life, I tend to justify the faulty thinking that because Jesus loves me, He should move in my timing.

But do you get it, Sis?

***Because* He loves us, He moves in His timing.**

Is there something in your life, even now, that you need to entrust to Him? An area where you think He should have moved already? Even more so, an area where you are questioning, "What's taking so long?" I want to encourage you to deal with the posture of your heart. Think about it in terms of agapao, the kind of love that does what's best for us. I know this is tough. I know you may have thoughts you don't even want to write down on paper. But I also know you won't be ready for what comes next if you don't. It's time to surrender, Sis. Go ahead. He's listening.

Day 4

Read John 11:1–44 (NASB). As you read, underline divine acts of God, moves of the Holy Spirit, anything supernatural with blue. Use yellow to highlight any words that God impresses upon your heart.

Now a certain man was sick: Lazarus of Bethany, the village of Mary and her sister Martha. And it was the Mary who anointed the Lord with ointment, and wiped His feet with her hair, whose brother Lazarus was sick. So the sisters sent word to Him, saying, "Lord, behold, he whom You love is sick." But when Jesus heard this, He said, "This sickness is not meant for death, but is for the glory of God, so that the Son of God may be glorified by it." (Now Jesus loved Martha and her sister, and Lazarus.) So when He heard that he was sick, He then stayed two days longer in the place where He was. Then after this He said to the disciples, "Let's go to Judea again." The disciples said to Him, "Rabbi, the Jews were just now seeking to stone You, and yet You are going there again?" Jesus replied, "Are there not twelve hours in the day? If anyone walks during the day, he does not stumble, because he sees the light of this world. But if anyone walks during the night, he stumbles, because the light is not in him." This He said, and after this He said to them, "Our friend Lazarus has fallen asleep; but I am going so that I may awaken him from sleep." The disciples then said to Him, "Lord, if he has fallen asleep, he will come out of it." Now Jesus had spoken of his death, but they thought that He was speaking about actual sleep. So Jesus then said to them plainly, "Lazarus died, and I am glad for your sakes that I was not there, so that you may believe; but let's go to him." Therefore Thomas, who was called Didymus, said to his fellow disciples, "Let's also go, so that we may die with Him!" So when Jesus came, He found that he had already been in the tomb four days. Now Bethany was near Jerusalem, about fifteen stadia away; and many of the Jews had come to Martha and Mary, to console them about their brother. So then Martha, when she heard that Jesus was coming, went to meet Him, but Mary stayed in the house. Martha then said to Jesus, "Lord, if You had been here, my brother would not have died. Even now I know that whatever You ask of God, God will give You." Jesus

said to her, "Your brother will rise from the dead." Martha said to Him, "I know that he will rise in the resurrection on the last day." Jesus said to her, "I am the resurrection and the life; the one who believes in Me will live, even if he dies, and everyone who lives and believes in Me will never die. Do you believe this?" She said to Him, "Yes, Lord; I have come to believe that You are the Christ, the Son of God, and He who comes into the world." When she had said this, she left and called Mary her sister, saying secretly, "The Teacher is here and is calling for you." And when she heard this, she got up quickly and came to Him. Now Jesus had not yet come into the village, but was still in the place where Martha met Him. Then the Jews who were with her in the house and were consoling her, when they saw that Mary had gotten up quickly and left, they followed her, thinking that she was going to the tomb to weep there. So when Mary came to the place where Jesus was, she saw Him and fell at His feet, saying to Him, "Lord, if You had been here, my brother would not have died." Therefore when Jesus saw her weeping, and the Jews who came with her also weeping, He was deeply moved in spirit and was troubled, and He said, "Where have you laid him?" They said to Him, "Lord, come and see." Jesus wept. So the Jews were saying, "See how He loved him!" But some of them said, "Could this man, who opened the eyes of the man who was blind, not have also kept this man from dying?" So Jesus, again being deeply moved within, came to the tomb. Now it was a cave, and a stone was lying against it. Jesus said, "Remove the stone." Martha, the sister of the deceased, said to Him, "Lord, by this time there will be a stench, for he has been dead four days." Jesus said to her, "Did I not say to you that if you believe, you will see the glory of God?" So they removed the stone. Then Jesus raised His eyes, and said, "Father, I thank You that You have heard Me. But I knew that You always hear Me; nevertheless, because of the people standing around I said it, so that they may believe that You sent Me." And when He had said these things, He cried out with a loud voice, "Lazarus, come forth." Out came the man who had died, bound hand and foot with wrappings, and his face was wrapped around with a cloth. Jesus said to them, "Unbind him, and let him go."

Use this space to write down any insights God gave you while reading through the passage.

Today I had you focus on looking for the things that only God could do. The supernatural. Moves of the Spirit. However you want to refer to it, we will studying this passage within the context of who Jesus was and what Jesus did.

We pick up where we left off yesterday. Martha confronted Jesus, and He responded to her faith-filled statement that was pregnant with anger. In verse 23, what does Jesus say?

He doesn't mention her emotions toward Him. He doesn't respond to her lack of cultural obedience to the shivah. He only makes her a promise.

> *Your brother will rise again.*

Jesus promises life to that which is dead. Her response shows us something that would be easy to miss if we aren't careful. What does she reply? (vs 24)

She knew the the theology of resurrection, but she didn't know the *person* of resurrection. Even after spending so much time with Jesus, she still didn't know Him fully.

I know in my own life, even after spending so much time learning the theology of resurrection, I didn't know Jesus as **The Resurrection.**

Until we allow Him to speak into those places in our lives that we think are dead, there will be aspects of Jesus—who He is—that we cannot know.

Martha had spent time with Him—a lot of time. She had served Him, and served alongside Him. Her family was in close relationship with Him. She even had faith that He was the healer. But this? She doesn't get this. Yet. Our emotions about the things we have watched die can get in the way of our belief in who He is.

Then Jesus explains. What does He say? (vs 25-26)

Jesus doesn't just resurrect things we thought were dead. He *is* the resurrection.

Martha knew from her Jewish faith that the dead would be resurrected upon judgement at the last day. But Jesus' response to her moved her from head knowledge to heart knowledge.

He is the One who fulfills the promises the Jews were waiting on.

How many of us are like Martha? We understand things because we have been taught them. Jesus is the redeemer. The restorer. The healer.

But when life hits, we can sometimes fall into the trap of longing for "one day." We forget that He is not just the God of tomorrow. He is the God of today. In your sorrow. In your grief. In your loss. In your disappointment. In your pain.

Martha realizes this. We see her move to recognizing who He is in one of the most bold proclamations of His Lordship that we see in all of Scripture. What does she confess? (vs 27)

Martha now believes in a different way and knows Jesus in a different way than she had previously. Why? How does knowing that Jesus *is* the resurrection change the way you view Him? Or view your relationship with Him?

Martha confesses the reality of who Jesus is in the face of her personal tragedy. This in and of itself is such an expression of her faith in Him that it changes their very relationship.

When you encounter Jesus as a person, allowing Him into those broken spaces, you come to know Him in a different way than you had previously. When you experience Him in the surrender of your sorrow, the things you thought were dead start to heal. That's how He breathes new life into us.

Do you believe that? Do you believe Him? Write the question Jesus asks at the end of verse 26.

____

Now, let me ask you the same question. Do you believe this? Do you believe that Jesus is The Resurrection? Do you believe Him when He speaks the only words that can truly heal your heart? Do you need some time with this? Take all the time you need.

____

____

____

____

My hope is that you are in a place where you can answer honestly, "Yes, Lord, I believe you are the Christ." If you can't, then I think you should stop for today. Take some time to worship, to pray, and to listen. He's not going anywhere. In fact, Jesus is ready to meet you on the road. But He won't force you to come.

Let's not lose sight of what Martha is experiencing. Lazarus has been dead four days. I know that for some of you, it feels too late. But don't allow what you see in the physical to steal away your faith in the spiritual.

He reminds her…again. And He reminds us…again.

Resurrection is not just something Jesus does. It's who He is. Resurrection and life are not a sermon or even a Bible study. They are a person.

Jesus proves to them that He *is* the resurrection. He is the redeemer and restorer of all things. Don't lose sight of that. Just because we don't see it in our timing, doesn't mean that it isn't happening.

Day 5

Read John 11:1–44 (NASB). As you read, underline any verbs, the action words, in pink. Use yellow to highlight any words that God impresses upon your heart.

Now a certain man was sick: Lazarus of Bethany, the village of Mary and her sister Martha. And it was the Mary who anointed the Lord with ointment, and wiped His feet with her hair, whose brother Lazarus was sick. So the sisters sent word to Him, saying, "Lord, behold, he whom You love is sick." But when Jesus heard this, He said, "This sickness is not meant for death, but is for the glory of God, so that the Son of God may be glorified by it." (Now Jesus loved Martha and her sister, and Lazarus.) So when He heard that he was sick, He then stayed two days longer in the place where He was. Then after this He said to the disciples, "Let's go to Judea again." The disciples said to Him, "Rabbi, the Jews were just now seeking to stone You, and yet You are going there again?" Jesus replied, "Are there not twelve hours in the day? If anyone walks during the day, he does not stumble, because he sees the light of this world. But if anyone walks during the night, he stumbles, because the light is not in him." This He said, and after this He said to them, "Our friend Lazarus has fallen asleep; but I am going so that I may awaken him from sleep." The disciples then said to Him, "Lord, if he has fallen asleep, he will come out of it." Now Jesus had spoken of his death, but they thought that He was speaking about actual sleep. So Jesus then said to them plainly, "Lazarus died, and I am glad for your sakes that I was not there, so that you may believe; but let's go to him." Therefore Thomas, who was called Didymus, said to his fellow disciples, "Let's also go, so that we may die with Him!" So when Jesus came, He found that he had already been in the tomb four days. Now Bethany was near Jerusalem, about fifteen stadia away; and many of the Jews had come to Martha and Mary, to console them about their brother. So then Martha, when she heard that Jesus was coming, went to meet Him, but Mary stayed in the house. Martha then said to Jesus, "Lord, if You had been here, my brother would not have died. Even now I know that whatever You ask of God, God will give You." Jesus

said to her, "Your brother will rise from the dead." Martha said to Him, "I know that he will rise in the resurrection on the last day." Jesus said to her, "I am the resurrection and the life; the one who believes in Me will live, even if he dies, and everyone who lives and believes in Me will never die. Do you believe this?" She said to Him, "Yes, Lord; I have come to believe that You are the Christ, the Son of God, and He who comes into the world." When she had said this, she left and called Mary her sister, saying secretly, "The Teacher is here and is calling for you." And when she heard this, she got up quickly and came to Him. Now Jesus had not yet come into the village, but was still in the place where Martha met Him. Then the Jews who were with her in the house and were consoling her, when they saw that Mary had gotten up quickly and left, they followed her, thinking that she was going to the tomb to weep there. So when Mary came to the place where Jesus was, she saw Him and fell at His feet, saying to Him, "Lord, if You had been here, my brother would not have died." Therefore when Jesus saw her weeping, and the Jews who came with her also weeping, He was deeply moved in spirit and was troubled, and He said, "Where have you laid him?" They said to Him, "Lord, come and see." Jesus wept. So the Jews were saying, "See how He loved him!" But some of them said, "Could this man, who opened the eyes of the man who was blind, not have also kept this man from dying?" So Jesus, again being deeply moved within, came to the tomb. Now it was a cave, and a stone was lying against it. Jesus said, "Remove the stone." Martha, the sister of the deceased, said to Him, "Lord, by this time there will be a stench, for he has been dead four days." Jesus said to her, "Did I not say to you that if you believe, you will see the glory of God?" So they removed the stone. Then Jesus raised His eyes, and said, "Father, I thank You that You have heard Me. But I knew that You always hear Me; nevertheless, because of the people standing around I said it, so that they may believe that You sent Me." And when He had said these things, He cried out with a loud voice, "Lazarus, come forth." Out came the man who had died, bound hand and foot with wrappings, and his face was wrapped around with a cloth. Jesus said to them, "Unbind him, and let him go."

Use this space to write down any insights God gave you while reading through the passage.

Today is our last day for the week. I know this part of our study has been a little heavy, but I'm not sorry. I want you to get this—to *really* get it. We are going to finish up with the best part of the story today. Ready? Me too!

Martha, after coming to realize who Jesus was—who He *really* was—is with Jesus at the tomb of her brother. As Jesus starts to move, she starts to argue in true Martha fashion about what Jesus is about to do. What does she say? (vs 39)

And do you know what I love about this part? The way Jesus responds. What does He say to her? (vs 40)

He reminds her of His promise to her. I can't tell you how many times I have felt like I have learned something about an aspect of the character of Jesus, only to be overtaken by my emotions later. (I told you I am a Martha.) She sees what is going on in the physical, and it clouds her idea of what can happen in the spiritual. But do you know what else I love? Again, how Jesus responds.

What happens in response? (vs 41)

Jesus does what He set out to do. Why? Because resurrection isn't something He does, it's who He is. The stone was rolled away, and Jesus speaks life into Lazarus' dead body.

You see, Jesus is working, despite our thoughts on the matter. With or without our belief or help, He is going to be at work. Again, it's who He is. We can either acknowledge it and be a part of what He is doing, or we can question it. Either way, Jesus is who He says He is.

After Lazarus comes out of the cave, Jesus does something else that I want to make sure you catch. What does Jesus tell them? (vs 44)

Jesus plays a role in our miracle, and we also play a role. Lazarus needed to be unwrapped. Sometimes we need to unwrap our miracle. Sometimes we need to acknowledge it, work through it, and realize it may not even look like we thought it would. For me, that happens through time in prayer, asking the Lord to speak into those areas of my life where I can sense some healing.

What are some ways you can unwrap your miracle? Are there things that come to mind?

As we end our time focusing on Martha's role and response in this story, I want to leave you with a couple of things to think about over the weekend. We will revisit some of this story next week as we study Mary, but I want you to pray about some key points in the meantime.

Because Jesus is The Resurrection, He will redeem and restore things in your life if you will let Him. It's who He is. Our role is to share those things with others. When the world sees the restoration of the things that were dead in your life, they will respond to the One who restores.

Make a plan to share with at least three people what God is doing in your life and what you are learning. Write down their names here.

As I have mentioned before, this is the last miracle Jesus performs before His death. In a culture where women are not permitted to be a witness in a court of law, Jesus chooses to perform this miracle in such a way that two women become part of the testimony itself. In addition, we see Martha declare who Jesus is in one of the most profound and bold statements of the identity of Jesus in all of Scripture.

Why? Because when He speaks to her—despite her impulsive and emotional self—*she hears.*

CHAPTER FIVE

Mary of Bethany

A Woman of Discipleship • John 12:1–8 (NIV®)

This week, we are continuing our two part study with Mary, the sister of Martha. As a reminder, just like last week, we need to carry two things in our hearts as we study. Mary is one of three siblings who had a special friendship with Jesus. But Mary herself, apart from Martha and even her brother Lazarus, had a unique relationship with the Lord. I think that, in and of itself, holds so much value for us as believers. As women, we can sometimes be quick to identify ourselves within the context of our relationships. As much as we value those roles, we are also more than someone's mom, wife, or daughter. We are loved uniquely, created uniquely, and purposed uniquely. There is so much value in who we are, Sis. Let's keep that close this week.

Day 1

Read John 12:1–8 (NIV®). As you read, underline any names in green. Use yellow to highlight any words that God impresses upon your heart.

Six days before the Passover, Jesus came to Bethany, where Lazarus lived, whom Jesus had raised from the dead. Here a dinner was given in Jesus' honor. Martha served, while Lazarus was among those reclining at the table with him. Then Mary took about a pint of pure nard, an expensive perfume; she poured it on Jesus' feet and wiped his feet with her hair. And the house was filled with the fragrance of the perfume. But one of his disciples, Judas Iscariot, who was later to betray him, objected, "Why wasn't this perfume sold and the money given to the poor? It was worth a year's wages." He did not say this because he cared about the poor but because he was a thief; as keeper of the money bag, he used to help himself to what was put into it. "Leave her alone," Jesus replied. "It was intended that she should save this perfume for the day of my burial. You will always have the poor among you, but you will not always have me."

Use this space to write down any insights God gave you while reading through the passage.

So many of the things we studied last week about Martha are also true of Mary. Before we dive into the new text for the week, I want to spend a little time looking at Mary's perspective in contrast to the way we studied Martha's last week. To do that, let's look back at that first story we considered at the beginning of our Martha study. Read through Luke 10:38–42 (NASB).

> *Now as they were traveling along, He entered a village; and a woman named Martha welcomed Him into her home. And she had a sister called Mary, who was also seated at the Lord's feet, and was listening to His word. But Martha was distracted with all her preparations; and she came up to Him and said, "Lord, do You not care that my sister has left me to do the serving by myself? Then tell her to help me." But the Lord answered and said to her, "Martha, Martha, you are worried and distracted by many things; but only one thing is necessary; for Mary has chosen the good part, which shall not be taken away from her.*

The first time we see Mary of Bethany, she is seated at the Lord's feet. As you now know from last week's study, sometimes that irritated me when I read it. My tendency was to always side with Martha. But again, we are reading these narratives with fresh perspective. So, in order to do that, we have to consider a couple of things about Mary.

Mary was most likely the younger of the two sisters. We explained last week that most scholars agree Martha owned her own home. In addition, Martha's name is often placed before Mary's when written in the text. This was a way the authors of Scripture used to portray the age of someone, from oldest to youngest. Also, as you may remember from last week, the expectation was probably that she should be helping with the preparations as part of the host family. Yet, here we see young, sweet Mary, sitting at the feet of Jesus. She likely knows that she should be in the kitchen helping, yet the Teacher was here. Sitting and listening to Him was the place she wanted to be most.

One other little tidbit? As a rabbi, Jesus would have been sitting at a low table or on a pillow on the ground. The disciples would sit around the rabbi to learn what He was teaching. The phrase "sit at his feet" actually meant to learn from a rabbi.

Look up Acts 22:3 and see if you notice any similarity. Write the verse here.

___

___

___

Did you catch it? Paul learned from Gamaliel in the same way. So, the fact that Mary was "seated at the Lord's feet" is an expression used to describe Mary as a disciple. And how does Jesus respond to her? He welcomes her. Anyone who says women have no place serving in ministry does not fully understand how Jesus operated. Not only do we see Jesus welcoming women and including them, but quite often He commissions them to do the work of telling others about Him. As we move into the rest of our study, remember the posture of Mary's heart: a disciple.

Flash back to the text of John 11 that we studied last week. From studying, you know that Mary handled her grief differently than Martha did. As a reminder, read John 11:20 and write down the difference in the way each handled themselves when they heard Jesus was approaching.

When they heard that Jesus was approaching Bethany, Martha went out to meet him, but Mary sat still in the house. Given the context of what we now know about Mary, how does that change your opinion on what happened? Remember when we talked about sitting shivah?

Write down any insights you may now have about Mary and her grief.

By staying inside the house, sitting in her grief, Mary was actually following the religious and cultural custom. The fact that she was a disciple of Jesus helps us to understand that perhaps she knew she should stay put. Martha was the more brazen one, dropping everything to go out and confront Jesus with her aggressive, though faith-filled, words.

What happens next is one of my favorite aspects of this entire storyline of Scripture. Martha, still in her own grief, comes back to the house and says something to Mary. What does she say? (vs 28)

Here is the verse in the King James Version because I like how almost poetic it sounds:

The Master is come, and calleth for thee. John 11:28 (KJV)

Mary is sitting in her grief, her anger, and her religion. Yet Jesus pursues her and asks her to leave that place and come to Him.

Oh, Sis. Do you realize those words are for you too?

Grief has become familiar to me. In the last couple of years, I suffered not only the loss of both my grandparents who raised me, but also experienced a failed adoption. Grief almost feels like a friend.

Sorrow is an emotion most people are not comfortable with, yet it's a normal response to loss. For me, as a mom and a ministry leader, I have felt like I didn't have enough time even to grieve. I'm not saying that I didn't have an appropriate amount of time off when those events happened. But the thing is, society almost expects us to have our grieving time within a week or so, and then move on and get back to life as normal. Except there is nothing normal about how you feel when you are grieving. For me, grief has always felt like waves. I have moments of calm, even calm days, but then these big waves come. As time goes on, the waves get farther apart, but they still come. Sometimes I feel like Mary, content to sit on the floor in my room, surrounded by sorrow and heartbreak. It's easier than walking my grief out. It's easier than confrontation or anger. My faith tells me those things are not appropriate, so instead I sit.

That place is not where Jesus wants us. Hidden. Alone. Broken. Instead, He comes for us.

The Master has come, and calls for you.
In your grief, the Master has come, and calls for you.
In your pain, the Master has come, and calls for you.
In your doubt, the Master has come, and calls for you.
In your fear, the Master has come, and calls for you.
In your anger, the Master has come, and calls for you.
In your anxiety, the Master has come, and calls for you.

Sis, no matter where you are sitting right now, the Master has come, and He is calling for you. Do you hear Him?

I want you to pay careful attention to what happens next.

Mary gets up and goes to meet Jesus.

When you hear Him calling, truly hear Him, you will be motivated to move toward Him. Sometimes we need to hear that from our sister. And if no one has ever said that to you, I am saying it to you now:

> *The Master has come, and calls for you.*

Is there someone you need to say that to? Take a few minutes to pray for someone the Lord drops in your heart. Maybe you are the one who needs this word right now. I know the first time I realized what the verse was truly saying, it brought tears to my eyes. Spend a little time in prayer, just reflecting on what this means. We will pick up with our new text for this week tomorrow. Praying for you, Sis.

Day 2

Read John 12:1–8 (NIV®). As you read, highlight any timing words (first, after, then, etc.) with purple. Use yellow to highlight any words that God impresses upon your heart.

Six days before the Passover, Jesus came to Bethany, where Lazarus lived, whom Jesus had raised from the dead. Here a dinner was given in Jesus' honor. Martha served, while Lazarus was among those reclining at the table with him. Then Mary took about a pint of pure nard, an expensive perfume; she poured it on Jesus' feet and wiped his feet with her hair. And the house was filled with the fragrance of the perfume. But one of his disciples, Judas Iscariot, who was later to betray him, objected, "Why wasn't this perfume sold and the money given to the poor? It was worth a year's wages." He did not say this because he cared about the poor but because he was a thief; as keeper of the money bag, he used to help himself to what was put into it. "Leave her alone," Jesus replied. "It was intended that she should save this perfume for the day of my burial. You will always have the poor among you, but you will not always have me."

Use this space to write down any insights God gave you while reading through the passage.

There's an older song called "Alabaster Box" that runs through my head every time I read this passage. Maybe you're familiar with it. It was sung as a special in most churches at some point. And although I love the song, there are some parts in it that I want to make sure you take and put on the shelf for now. The song is about Mary washing the feet of Jesus both with oil and with her tears, referring to her as a sinful woman. The reason for this is there are some people who read the four foot washing scenes in the gospels and consider them all to be about the same woman. Don't know what I am talking about? Let me walk you through them.

Read through Matthew 26:6–13 and write down any differences you see between Matthew's version of things and John's.

Now read through Mark 14:3–11 and write down any differences you see.

These first three seem pretty similar, right? That's because they are. Scholars agree that these three accounts are all talking about the same thing. Now for the sake of the argument, you can read through Luke 7:36–50. There are too many differences to write them all down, but I think it will be helpful for you to read through it at least.

Now, when you are reading Luke 7:36–50, doesn't it feel different? Maybe you can't quite put your finger on it, because the actions and scene seem familiar. But the story from Luke isn't about Mary—it's about a different woman. They are in a different place—a different season of ministry for Jesus and His disciples—and even the reaction of Jesus is different. I was somewhat skeptical about that when I first started to study because there were aspects of this fourth story that seemed so similar. But once I thoroughly studied, I realized what the most likely reason was for that. To us, washing someone's feet is an odd thing to imagine. Very few churches still practice foot washing on a regular basis. Our church has done it on occasion, and I myself have had my feet washed both on missions trips and during my ordination ceremony. Neither felt normal or comfortable. In fact, one was a surprise and I didn't shave my legs first. That was super uncomfortable!

For us, this situation just *feels* awkward. It's natural for us to lump all these stories into one. But in the time and the culture that Jesus was ministering in, the act of foot washing was an everyday occurrence. It was expected as part of receiving someone into your home. It was as common as offering someone a glass of water. The reason? Think of the types of shoes the people wore. Sandals. What was on the roads? Dust, sometimes animal excrement. Sometimes human excrement. Their feet got pretty nasty. So, when they arrived home or went to someone's house, the washing of the feet was a job reserved for slaves or the lowest member of the household. Their feet were the dirtiest part of their bodies.

Given this information, read through John 13:1–17. After reading, write down any new insights you have about this scene.

Washing the feet of the disciples was symbolic of Jesus' love, devotion, and sacrifice. Taking the position of a servant, Jesus took the dirtiest part of them, symbolically, and restored them so they were clean again. He does the same thing with our hearts, if only we let Him.

Have you let Him? Is there something that is rising to the surface in you right now? Yes, this fourth story may not be Mary. But she is included, and I think the reason may be because we can see ourselves in her. I know I can. I am that sinful woman, coming to Jesus with my tears, over and over again. And you know what? He responds with nothing but love and grace and forgiveness. Every. Single. Time. Reflect on that if you need to. I think it's important to process whatever may be going through your heart and mind right now.

So, now that we have established that Mary was not the "sinful woman" in Luke, we can focus on who she was: a disciple. We can also focus on what she was doing.

We have already talked about how foot washing was a regular part of life within this culture. But Mary's story is made famous for a reason. There are a couple of points I want to make about what was actually happening.

Normally, foot washings were done with water. In this text, however, Mary used perfume. Perfume in this culture was not the watery stuff we have now. What does the text call Mary's perfume?

Pure nard was expensive—the verse even tells us so—but I want you to realize how expensive. Nard is an oil from the root of the nard plant, which was not native to the area. The nard would sometimes be mixed with myron, which was a base of olive oil mixed with other aromatic substances. It was from the northern mountains in India and would have been imported at a high cost. In fact, it cost the equivalent of about a year's wages for an average worker.

In addition, the size of the jar also tells us how expensive it would have been. A half pint was an incredible amount, even just in volume. A more normal amount would have been around half an ounce, perhaps an ounce at most. Because of both the cost and the potency of the fragrance, such a large amount was very unusual. This could possibly have been a family heirloom that was passed down for generations. We have some things like that in our family. Even that fact brings extra personal value for Mary.

Also, remember where they were—Bethany. What does Bethany mean?

This was an incredibly rare and valuable jar of oil for Mary.

Now that we understand that this perfume was not like a spray from Bath and Body Works, let's read through this scene one more time. Actually, go back to the version from Mark that I had you read before: Mark 14:1–9. Pay special attention to verse 8.

Did you see it? What does Jesus say about Mary in verse 8?

She used what she had, and she did what she could. Mary was in all likelihood a young girl from a poor town. She didn't have many resources. She didn't have much time. What we see here is an act of devotion, and the sacrifice of something precious to her to show her love to Jesus. And she did it in a way that was incredibly humble, not caring what anyone around her thought. In fact, she was the only one in the room who washed the feet of the Master.

I have felt that way before. The only woman disciple, surrounded by men, and I am doing something they would find foolish. Yet my heart desired only to be obedient, to serve, to do what I could—even if others thought it was foolish or wasteful. Their opinions were not what mattered to me; only His.

Sis, nothing is ever wasted on Jesus. No gift, no matter how big or how small, is ever wasted when we give it to Jesus. Our money, our resources, our talent, our time.... Nothing is wasted in the kingdom.

It's time for me to get a little personal here. I think it will help you understand where I am coming from.

For a little over five years of my life, my husband and I worked tirelessly to bring home a little boy through adoption from an African country. Countless trips, lawyers, home studies, court cases. It's a very long story, but I will tell you that we do not have that child in our home. A child that I loved, that I fought for, that we spent tens of thousands of dollars to bring to the States. Because of some very deceptive and evil people, my arms are empty. I thought they would be filled with a beautiful little boy named Gideon.

I poured out my oil. Others told me how foolish I was for wasting so much money and time. For not giving up. For fighting for justice.

But Jesus? He defended my offering. He saw my heart, and He has worked that raw and tender space into something beautiful. I am now working with orphans in Africa in several countries, and I work from a place of love and compassion for them in a way that I would not have had if I had not gone through what I did with Gideon.

Do you see it, Sis?

Nothing in the kingdom is ever wasted. When we pour out our oil for Him, He defends us. Nothing is wasted on Jesus.

Use this space to process anything you need to. I know I'm going to need it today.

Day 3

Read John 12:1–8 (NIV®). As you read, circle any numbers with orange. Use yellow to highlight any words that God impresses upon your heart.

Six days before the Passover, Jesus came to Bethany, where Lazarus lived, whom Jesus had raised from the dead. Here a dinner was given in Jesus' honor. Martha served, while Lazarus was among those reclining at the table with him. Then Mary took about a pint of pure nard, an expensive perfume; she poured it on Jesus' feet and wiped his feet with her hair. And the house was filled with the fragrance of the perfume. But one of his disciples, Judas Iscariot, who was later to betray him, objected, "Why wasn't this perfume sold and the money given to the poor? It was worth a year's wages." He did not say this because he cared about the poor but because he was a thief; as keeper of the money bag, he used to help himself to what was put into it. "Leave her alone," Jesus replied. "It was intended that she should save this perfume for the day of my burial. You will always have the poor among you, but you will not always have me."

Use this space to write down any insights God gave you while reading through the passage.

Today we are going to spend a little time looking at the actual act that we see Mary perform in this portion of Scripture—the anointing.

In the culture we are talking about, anointing was symbolic in many ways. Often, people were anointed—meaning they were set apart—for a specific task or role. We have similar roles in our culture, although it looks a little different. Senior Pastor. Missionary. Youth Pastor. Hospice Chaplain. People who are set apart to do a specific job, fulfill a specific role, given to them by God.

In the Jewish culture, this "setting apart" would be accompanied by an actual anointing with oil. Kings, priests, and sometimes a special guest who was placed in a seat of honor would be anointed for their role. If someone was referred to as anointed, usually the person being discussed was the high priest. The high priest was the one who was acting as a redeemer for the people's sins, offering the sacrifice in the temple. The oil was normally poured on the priest's head, and because priests wore linen robes, the oil would flow down over them and flow out from them instead of being absorbed. So "the anointing" would flow from them in a way that others could see, touch, and feel.

In the Old Testament, the promised coming king was referred to as the Messiah, which is a Hebrew word. In the New Testament, the Hebrew was translated into the Greek as "Christos." Christ.

Do you know what that means? Any guesses? ______________________________

Anointed King

Christ is not the last name of Jesus. Christ is His position. He is the One set apart to redeem God's people through sacrifice. When Mary chose to use the oil to anoint Jesus, starting with His head and moving down to His feet, she was making a public declaration about who she believed Him to be. The Redeemer. He was *her* redeemer. This moment was first about who He was for her.

What does it say about how Mary wiped up the oil? (vs 3)

____

Ever thought about what that may mean? In that culture, a woman's hair represented her glory, her self-worth. Women didn't normally let their hair down in public. She was laying her glory down at the feet of Jesus. This was her act of worship to Him.

Isn't that such a beautiful picture? Unfortunately, not everyone in the room agreed.

How does Judas respond? (vs 5) ______________________________

____

What happens next is something that I absolutely love. Jesus responds to Judas. What does He say in the first part of verse 7?

____

____

Leave her alone.

Your sacrifice. Your oil. Your relationship. First and foremost, your service to Jesus is about your relationship with Him and your response to who you believe Him to be, regardless of what anyone else thinks. When Jesus sees our heart in that, He will defend us against those who would speak out against it.

Another aspect of the anointing that we need to consider is the timeframe. What was about to happen in the coming days?

____

And what does Jesus say in the second part of verse 7?______________________________

____

The word "save" in the original text is the word *tereo*. It means so much more than simply to rescue or keep something safe. The connotation of the word here is to guard at the level of a prison guard who is responsible for keeping watch. It's about long-term obedience as part of the "saving" process.

This wasn't just some old family oil that had been collecting dust on a shelf. It was intended for this purpose, just as Mary was intended for this purpose.

In this culture, there was also another kind of anointing. It was part of the burial process. The anointing would be part of the cleaning and preparing of the body. They would use oil and spices as part of the washing.

Think back to the gifts that were brought to baby Jesus by the wise men. What were they? Gold, ____________________ and ____________________.

Frankincense and myrrh were burial spices. The anointing oil that Mary used was a type of myrrh.

What is the significance of this, do you think?

____

____

Both of these instances were a foreshadowing of what was to come.

When the time came, the men who would bring the body of Jesus down off the cross would have to work quickly and would not be able to fulfill the traditional practice of washing and anointing Jesus' body before putting Him in the tomb.

There is some power there, Sis. The only anointing Jesus would receive came from a woman disciple.

Does that hit you the way it hits me? Take some time to process in your heart the things we discovered today, and realize that our service and sacrifice to Jesus are significant.

____

____

____

____

Day 4

Read John 12:1–8 (NIV®). As you read, underline divine acts of God, moves of the Holy Spirit, anything supernatural with blue. Use yellow to highlight any words that God impresses upon your heart.

Six days before the Passover, Jesus came to Bethany, where Lazarus lived, whom Jesus had raised from the dead. Here a dinner was given in Jesus' honor. Martha served, while Lazarus was among those reclining at the table with him. Then Mary took about a pint of pure nard, an expensive perfume; she poured it on Jesus' feet and wiped his feet with her hair. And the house was filled with the fragrance of the perfume. But one of his disciples, Judas Iscariot, who was later to betray him, objected, "Why wasn't this perfume sold and the money given to the poor? It was worth a year's wages." He did not say this because he cared about the poor but because he was a thief; as keeper of the money bag, he used to help himself to what was put into it. "Leave her alone," Jesus replied. "It was intended that she should save this perfume for the day of my burial. You will always have the poor among you, but you will not always have me."

Use this space to write down any insights God gave you while reading through the passage.

When I was young, my grandmother had a collection of very rare and expensive old perfume bottles. She had collected them over the years, and many were antiques. Some were French; some were Italian. They were beautiful, and we weren't supposed to touch them. But of course I did. I used to open them up, so I could smell them. One time, I accidentally spilled one, so I filled it up with water, hoping Nana wouldn't notice. She did.

As a child, I remember watching as Nana painstakingly cleaned the dust off of each tiny bottle. They were very valuable and precious to her. As she placed them all back on the mirrored tray, she reminded me not to touch them. No sooner had she left than I was already opening the pink one. Just to smell it. I was careful not to spill it, but even holding the lid in my hands was enough. The fragrance hung in the air. I washed my hands carefully, two times with warm water and soap, and then went downstairs for lunch. As soon as I did, I was caught. The aroma of the perfume gave me away.

Today we are going to consider the consequence of the anointing that Mary performed for Jesus. This may sound odd at first, but we need to take a look at the broader picture of what was happening.

What kind of jar held the oil Mary used? You will have to refer to the supportive stories from the additional gospels to find the answer.

____

An alabaster jar. Some translations say box, but in the original text, that word meant flask or long-necked jar. The first time I saw alabaster, it surprised me. It was dense and hard like marble. I have an alabaster ball that I keep on my desk to remind me of this story actually. I like to pick it up and hold it. It's heavy and solid. The way those jars were made, she would need to break the jar in order to access the oil. Once it was opened, the perfume would have to be used. There was no way to save some of it to use another time.

That aspect speaks to me. I get the sense that God has given me a special gift to be used only on Jesus. What does that look like in your own life? How is that relevant for you?

____

____

____

____

____

One of the things I hope you are starting to see is that the stories of these women speak to our own stories. The things we see and learn about how Jesus interacted with them shows us how He longs to interact with us. I am so thankful for the gift of God's Word.

Let's keep going.

When we are talking about anointing, specifically of a king, the king would receive the anointing as part of the coronation ceremony instead of a crown. The oil that was used to anoint Hebrew kings was precious, expensive, and used for the specific purpose of giving off an almost holy aroma. The people around them would inhale this special fragrance, and it would signify royalty to them. In fact, kings were judged not only by how they looked in their royal clothing but also by how they smelled with their royal aroma. The clothes they wore would even be fragranced so that their aroma could be recognized during special occasions.

Let's look up a couple of examples. Write out the relevant portions of these next few verses.

Psalm 45:7–8

Song of Songs 3:6–7

1 Kings 1:38–40

2 Corinthians 2:14–16

We can clearly see examples of the importance of anointing throughout the Scriptures. I especially love the last one, though. Go ahead and read it again. The verse says that God…

> *uses us to spread the aroma of the knowledge of him everywhere.* (2 Corinthians 2:14, NIV®)

Don't you love that part? Our obedience is to sit at His feet, be His disciple, and learn from Him. Then as we pour out our gifting at the feet of Jesus, we are enabled to spread the aroma of His fragrance in a way that other people can see who Jesus is—The King.

Do you remember what was coming the next day—after this scene where Jesus was anointed?

Read the rest of John 12 and write down any new insights you may have now.

____

____

____

____

____

Jesus would be headed into Jerusalem. What would the people declare Him? (vs 13)

____

Isn't it interesting that this impromptu processional, where people declared Jesus king, appropriately includes the royal aroma of a king as Jesus walks past them? The oil Mary used to anoint Jesus was so pungent that the fragrance would likely have clung to Him for quite a while. The aroma would linger in a way that others would smell it wherever He went.

As He entered Jerusalem on a donkey.
In the garden.
During His arrest.
When He was before Pilate.
When He was stripped naked and beaten.
When He was nailed to a cross.

Jesus was the anointed King, with the true aroma of a king, set apart to redeem His people through sacrifice. As He hung on a cross, others would sense who He was—even if they didn't quite understand it yet.

There's more. Go ahead and write out 2 Corinthians 2:15. Note any thoughts you have as you read the verse out loud.

Just as that aroma clung to Him, it now clings to us. The fragrance of Jesus, His royalty, has now been transferred to us as His children. We are daughters of the King! The Bible says that because of Jesus, we are now an aroma to God—the aroma of Christ. Christos, the anointed King. No longer do we bear the stench of our own sin. Instead, we bear the fragrance of royalty. Thank You, Jesus.

Take some time to write a prayer of thankfulness for how Jesus transforms our sacrifice for His glory. Remember, nothing is wasted in the kingdom, Sis.

Day 5

Read John 12:1–8 (NIV®). As you read, underline all the verbs, the action words, in pink. Use yellow to highlight any words that God impresses upon your heart.

Six days before the Passover, Jesus came to Bethany, where Lazarus lived, whom Jesus had raised from the dead. Here a dinner was given in Jesus' honor. Martha served, while Lazarus was among those reclining at the table with him. Then Mary took about a pint of pure nard, an expensive perfume; she poured it on Jesus' feet and wiped his feet with her hair. And the house was filled with the fragrance of the perfume. But one of his disciples, Judas Iscariot, who was later to betray him, objected, "Why wasn't this perfume sold and the money given to the poor? It was worth a year's wages." He did not say this because he cared about the poor but because he was a thief; as keeper of the money bag, he used to help himself to what was put into it. "Leave her alone," Jesus replied. "It was intended that she should save this perfume for the day of my burial. You will always have the poor among you, but you will not always have me."

Use this space to write down any insights God gave you while reading through the passage.

Well, we made it to Day 5, Sis. I'm so proud of you. We had a lot to work through this week. Today will be less study heavy and more reflection. I want to provide this space for you to think through, pray, journal, and process. I just have a couple of thoughts to guide this time.

1. Where are you seated?

When we first see Mary, she is seated at the feet of Jesus, listening to Him teach.

When we see Mary in the Lazarus story, she is seated in her grief.

When Mary meets Jesus after He has called to her in her grief, she falls to the ground, seated at His feet in surrender and sorrow.

When we last see Mary, she is seated at the feet of Jesus, pouring out her sacrifice in an act of worship.

Throughout our study of Mary, we see her seated. Her story begins and ends with being seated at the feet of Jesus. In between those moments, though, we see a much different side of her. What is the difference between the beginning and the ending? What emotions do you see in each of these scenes?

#1 ______________________________

____

#2 ______________________________

____

#3 ______________________________

____

#4 ______________________________

____

Do you see a difference? What does that mean for us? Where are you seated right now? How does that impact your emotions? What can we learn from Mary as we apply that to our own lives?

____

____

____

____

2. Jesus is our defender.

How do we see Jesus respond in His first encounter with Mary? (Luke 10:42)

How do we see Jesus respond in the last story of Mary? (John 12:7)

In both of these scenes, Jesus defends Mary. Sis, let me tell you something.

Jesus is your defender too. When our hearts are focused on Him, when we are obedient to Him, when we pour out our offering to Him, when we are grieving, or lost, or hurting…

He Is Our Defender.

What goes through your mind as you read those words? At what times in your life have you felt like you needed a defender? Now that you realize this, how will that change your heart, your mind, and your actions the next time you feel that familiar sting of judgement? Take a deep breath. I am laying down some life changing concepts here, but you are going to need to pick them up and take them with you.

He is our defender.

When Jesus defends her, *she hears.*

And it changes the way she lives.

Go ahead and take all the time you need. Praying for you as you allow these truths to sink in.

CHAPTER SIX

Mary Magdalene

A Woman of Response • John 20:1–18 (NLT)

It's our last week together, Sis. Bittersweet, isn't it? As much as I have enjoyed walking through the pages of Scripture together, I am so excited to get to this point. This chapter is going to be a little different from the previous ones. Until now, I have walked you through, bit by bit, to show you what Jesus says to women and how He interacts with them.

Now? It's your turn. You are going to put together all the things we have been learning to see what the Lord tells *you*. Are you ready? I think you are.

We have spent the last five weeks learning the fundamentals of the Color Method of Bible study. Now it's time to put all of that learning together, so you can take this method of study past the pages of *She Hears*. My hope and prayer is that you have learned a little more about how God speaks to us through His Word.

This week, instead of focusing on one aspect of Scripture each day, you will do all of the aspects in one shot. The goal moving forward is that you can approach other portions of text this way, learning how to think through some of the things you may have otherwise skipped over. Also, please don't feel constrained to the aspects and colors I chose. Some people do twice as many colors, looking specifically for things like location, genre, adjectives, etc. These are just the ones that work for me in the amount of time I normally have to study. Feel free to make this process your own.

At this point, my hope is that you have a better understanding about how to examine the text in a way that allows the Holy Spirit to reveal what He wants you to hear. That's when you realize the "she" in the title, *She Hears*, is *you*. Yes, *you*, Sis. Although we have been learning about how other women heard from Jesus, I want you to realize He has a special message for *you*. The Word is living and active, which means you can read the same passage your entire life, yet the Lord can teach you something in a fresh way each time you read it. Isn't God amazing?

One more thing. As we work our way through this week, you will be studying the same chunk of Scripture each day, doing the full color method each day. The difference? You will be using different versions of the same text from various translations of the Bible. I don't know if you're like me, but I tend to favor one version over another. Yet I have discovered that sometimes the richness of the text in a different version touches my heart in a special way. I may have read the same text over and over, but the fifth time I read it, in a different version, God will pierce my heart with a fresh vision, thought, or act of obedience. I know this way of studying may not be for everyone, but I want you to at least experience it once, as we seek to see and understand what God is teaching us this week.

Before we start studying Mary Magdalene, I want to point out a couple of things to keep in mind as you study:

- Read through this Scripture with fresh eyes and a clean slate, like we have done with the other women. Regardless of whether you are reading and studying Mary Magdalene for the first time or the hundredth, approach the text with an open heart, ready to hear what the Lord would say to you.
- Consider looking for Mary Magdalene in other books of the Bible. I know I have done the leg work for you up until now, but it's time for you to figure this part out, so you can do it moving forward. Key places to look for additional information are cross references directly in the reading, the index in the back of your Bible, or online using a search like BibleGateway.com.
- If you don't already have one, consider purchasing a good Study Bible to help you in your understanding. Online tools are available as well, just make sure you are doing your own studying of the Word first. You want to hear what Jesus is telling *you* first, before you listen to what He told someone else.
- Common misconceptions about Mary: She was not a prostitute or romantically involved with Jesus. Scripture never says anything of the sort. It does say, however, the reasons why she loved Jesus so much. As you read and study, see if you can figure out what that was all about.

After today, I am not going to say a whole lot this week. I'll check back in with you at the end of the week. Listen to what God is saying. That's the whole point. As we have learned up until now, Jesus is intentional about His relationships with women. This week is no different. In fact, this is my absolute favorite chapter of the book. Why? Well…dig in and see for yourself!

Day 1

Read John 20:1–18 (NLT).

- ☐ As you read, underline any names in green.
- ☐ Highlight any timing words (first, after, then, etc.) with purple.
- ☐ Circle any numbers with orange.
- ☐ Underline divine acts of God, moves of the Holy Spirit, or anything supernatural with blue.
- ☐ Highlight all the verbs, the action words, in pink.
- ☐ Use yellow to highlight any words that God impresses upon your heart.

Early on Sunday morning, while it was still dark, Mary Magdalene came to the tomb and found that the stone had been rolled away from the entrance. She ran and found Simon Peter and the other disciple, the one whom Jesus loved. She said, "They have taken the Lord's body out of the tomb, and we don't know where they have put him!" Peter and the other disciple started out for the tomb. They were both running, but the other disciple outran Peter and reached the tomb first. He stooped and looked in and saw the linen wrappings lying there, but he didn't go in. Then Simon Peter arrived and went inside. He also noticed the linen wrappings lying there, while the cloth that had covered Jesus' head was folded up and lying apart from the other wrappings. Then the disciple who had reached the tomb first also went in, and he saw and believed—for until then they still hadn't understood the Scriptures that said Jesus must rise from the dead. Then they went home. Mary was standing outside the tomb crying, and as she wept, she stooped and looked in. She saw two white-robed angels, one sitting at the head and the other at the foot of the place where the body of Jesus had been lying. "Dear woman, why are you crying?" the angels asked her. "Because they have taken away my Lord," she replied, "and I don't know where they have put him." She turned to leave and saw someone standing there. It was Jesus, but she didn't recognize him. "Dear woman, why are you crying?" Jesus asked her. "Who are you looking for?" She thought he was the gardener. "Sir," she said, "if you have taken him away, tell me where you have put him, and I will go and get him." "Mary!" Jesus said. She turned to him and cried out, "Rabboni!" (which is Hebrew for "Teacher"). "Don't cling to me," Jesus said, "for I haven't yet ascended to the Father. But go find my brothers and tell them, 'I am ascending to my Father and your Father, to my God and your God.'" Mary Magdalene found the disciples and told them, "I have seen the Lord!" Then she gave them his message.

Day 2

Read John 20:1–18 (NASB)

- ☐ As you read, underline any names in green.
- ☐ Highlight any timing words (first, after, then, etc.) with purple.
- ☐ Circle any numbers with orange.
- ☐ Underline divine acts of God, moves of the Holy Spirit, or anything supernatural with blue.
- ☐ Highlight all the verbs, the action words, in pink.
- ☐ Use yellow to highlight any words that God impresses upon your heart.

Now on the first day of the week Mary Magdalene came early to the tomb, while it was still dark, and saw the stone already removed from the tomb. So she ran and came to Simon Peter and to the other disciple whom Jesus loved, and said to them, "They have taken the Lord from the tomb, and we do not know where they have put Him." So Peter and the other disciple left, and they were going to the tomb. The two were running together; and the other disciple ran ahead, faster than Peter, and came to the tomb first; and he stooped to look in, and saw the linen wrappings lying there; however he did not go in. So Simon Peter also came, following him, and he entered the tomb; and he looked at the linen wrappings lying there, and the face-cloth which had been on His head, not lying with the linen wrappings but folded up in a place by itself. So the other disciple who had first come to the tomb also entered then, and he saw and believed. For they did not yet understand the Scripture, that He must rise from the dead. So the disciples went away again to their own homes.But Mary was standing outside the tomb, weeping; so as she wept, she stooped to look into the tomb; and she saw two angels in white sitting, one at the head and one at the feet, where the body of Jesus had been lying. And they said to her, "Woman, why are you weeping?" She said to them, "Because they have taken away my Lord, and I do not know where they put Him." When she had said this, she turned around and saw Jesus standing there, and yet she did not know that it was Jesus. Jesus said to her, "Woman, why are you weeping? Whom are you seeking?" Thinking that He was the gardener, she said to Him, "Sir, if you have carried Him away, tell me where you put Him, and I will take Him away." Jesus said to her, "Mary!" She turned and said to Him in Hebrew, "Rabboni!" (which means, Teacher). Jesus said to her, "Stop clinging to Me, for I have not yet ascended to the Father; but go to My brothers and say to them, 'I am ascending to My Father and your Father, and My God and your God.'" Mary Magdalene came and announced to the disciples, "I have seen the Lord," and that He had said these things to her.

Day 3

Read John 20:1–18 (MSG)

- ☐ As you read, underline any names in green.
- ☐ Highlight any timing words (first, after, then, etc.) with purple.
- ☐ Circle any numbers with orange.
- ☐ Underline divine acts of God, moves of the Holy Spirit, or anything supernatural with blue.
- ☐ Highlight all the verbs, the action words, in pink.
- ☐ Use yellow to highlight any words that God impresses upon your heart.

Early in the morning on the first day of the week, while it was still dark, Mary Magdalene came to the tomb and saw that the stone was moved away from the entrance. She ran at once to Simon Peter and the other disciple, the one Jesus loved, breathlessly panting, "They took the Master from the tomb. We don't know where they've put him." Peter and the other disciple left immediately for the tomb. They ran, neck and neck. The other disciple got to the tomb first, outrunning Peter. Stooping to look in, he saw the pieces of linen cloth lying there, but he didn't go in. Simon Peter arrived after him, entered the tomb, observed the linen cloths lying there, and the kerchief used to cover his head not lying with the linen cloths but separate, neatly folded by itself. Then the other disciple, the one who had gotten there first, went into the tomb, took one look at the evidence, and believed. No one yet knew from the Scripture that he had to rise from the dead. The disciples then went back home. But Mary stood outside the tomb weeping. As she wept, she knelt to look into the tomb and saw two angels sitting there, dressed in white, one at the head, the other at the foot of where Jesus' body had been laid. They said to her, "Woman, why do you weep?" "They took my Master," she said, "and I don't know where they put him." After she said this, she turned away and saw Jesus standing there. But she didn't recognize him. Jesus spoke to her, "Woman, why do you weep? Who are you looking for?" She, thinking that he was the gardener, said, "Mister, if you took him, tell me where you put him so I can care for him." Jesus said, "Mary." Turning to face him, she said in Hebrew, "*Rabboni!*" meaning "Teacher!" Jesus said, "Don't cling to me, for I have not yet ascended to the Father. Go to my brothers and tell them, 'I ascend to my Father and your Father, my God and your God.'" Mary Magdalene went, telling the news to the disciples: "I saw the Master!" And she told them everything he said to her.

Day 4

Read John 20:1–18 (ESV).

- ☐ As you read, underline any names in green.
- ☐ Highlight any timing words (first, after, then, etc.) with purple.
- ☐ Circle any numbers with orange.
- ☐ Underline divine acts of God, moves of the Holy Spirit, or anything supernatural with blue.
- ☐ Highlight all the verbs, the action words, in pink.
- ☐ Use yellow to highlight any words that God impresses upon your heart.

Now on the first day of the week Mary Magdalene came to the tomb early, while it was still dark, and saw that the stone had been taken away from the tomb. So she ran and went to Simon Peter and the other disciple, the one whom Jesus loved, and said to them, "They have taken the Lord out of the tomb, and we do not know where they have laid him." So Peter went out with the other disciple, and they were going toward the tomb. Both of them were running together, but the other disciple outran Peter and reached the tomb first. And stooping to look in, he saw the linen cloths lying there, but he did not go in. Then Simon Peter came, following him, and went into the tomb. He saw the linen cloths lying there, and the face cloth, which had been on Jesus' head, not lying with the linen cloths but folded up in a place by itself. Then the other disciple, who had reached the tomb first, also went in, and he saw and believed; for as yet they did not understand the Scripture, that he must rise from the dead. Then the disciples went back to their homes. But Mary stood weeping outside the tomb, and as she wept she stooped to look into the tomb. And she saw two angels in white, sitting where the body of Jesus had lain, one at the head and one at the feet. They said to her, "Woman, why are you weeping?" She said to them, "They have taken away my Lord, and I do not know where they have laid him." Having said this, she turned around and saw Jesus standing, but she did not know that it was Jesus. Jesus said to her, "Woman, why are you weeping? Whom are you seeking?" Supposing him to be the gardener, she said to him, "Sir, if you have carried him away, tell me where you have laid him, and I will take him away." Jesus said to her, "Mary." She turned and said to him in Aramaic, "Rabboni!" (which means Teacher). Jesus said to her, "Do not cling to me, for I have not yet ascended to the Father; but go to my brothers and say to them, 'I am ascending to my Father and your Father, to my God and your God.'" Mary Magdalene went and announced to the disciples, "I have seen the Lord"—and that he had said these things to her.

Day 5

Read John 20:1–18 (TPT).

☐ As you read, underline any names in green.

☐ Highlight any timing words (first, after, then, etc.) with purple.

☐ Circle any numbers with orange.

☐ Underline divine acts of God, moves of the Holy Spirit, or anything supernatural with blue.

☐ Highlight all the verbs, the action words, in pink.

☐ Use yellow to highlight any words that God impresses upon your heart.

Very early Sunday morning, before sunrise, Mary Magdalene made her way to the tomb. And when she arrived she discovered that the stone that sealed the entrance to the tomb was moved away! So she went running as fast as she could to go tell Peter and the other disciple, the one Jesus loved. She told them, "They've taken the Lord's body from the tomb, and we don't know where he is!" Then Peter and the other disciple jumped up and ran to the tomb to go see for themselves. They started out together, but the other disciple outran Peter and reached the tomb first. He didn't enter the tomb, but peeked in, and saw only the linen cloths lying there. Then Peter came behind him and went right into the tomb. He too noticed the linen cloths lying there, but the burial cloth that had been on Jesus' head had been rolled up and placed separate from the other cloths. Then the other disciple who had reached the tomb first went in, and after one look, he believed! For until then they hadn't understood the Scriptures that prophesied that he was destined to rise from the dead. Puzzled, Peter and the other disciple then left and went back to their homes. Mary arrived back at the tomb, broken and sobbing. She stooped to peer inside, and through her tears she saw two angels in dazzling white robes, sitting where Jesus' body had been laid—one at the head and one at the feet! "Dear woman, why are you crying?" they asked. Mary answered, "They have taken away my Lord, and I don't know where they've laid him." Then she turned around to leave, and there was

Jesus standing in front of her, but she didn't realize that it was him! He said to her, "Dear woman, why are you crying? Who are you looking for?" Mary answered, thinking he was only the gardener, "Sir, if you have taken his body somewhere else, tell me, and I will go and..." "Mary," Jesus interrupted her. Turning to face him, she said, "Rabboni!" (Aramaic for "my teacher") Jesus cautioned her, "Mary, don't hold on to me now, for I haven't yet ascended to God, my Father. And he's not only my Father and God, but now he's your Father and your God! Now go to my brothers and tell them what I've told you, that I am ascending to my Father—and your Father, to my God—and your God!" Then Mary Magdalene left to inform the disciples of her encounter with Jesus. "I have seen the Lord!" she told them. And she gave them his message.

Well? How did you do? Did you find the process of the color method to be helpful? What things did you see that you might otherwise have overlooked? I am so looking forward to discussing this with you! If you haven't already, please consider joining our *She Hears* Facebook page for discussion, online Bible study, and community with other women longing to hear Jesus. You can also connect at the blog shehears.org.

Now that you have had the chance to study Mary on your own, I want to point out just a few things that I learned along the way. My hope is not to take away from your own study, but just to enrich the things you already learned.

As we briefly touched on earlier this week, there are some common misconceptions about Mary Magdalene. Many consider her to be a prostitute or a romantic partner of Jesus. Let me address those concerns in case you missed it in your own study. Scripture never even alludes to the fact that Mary was a prostitute. We see early on that Jesus healed her from demon possession of seven demons. Her relationship with Him was rooted in the healing she received from Him. Because of the place of her name when we see her mentioned in the various groups of women, we know that she was older than Mary, the mother of Jesus. So how did she get a bad rap? Well, we can basically blame the Church for that.

Back in 591, Pope Gregory gave a series of Easter sermons that equated Mary Magdalene, Mary of Bethany, and an unnamed "sinful woman" as the same person. This was a gross misrepresentation of Scripture and led to a widely held belief that she was promiscuous or a prostitute. That simply is not the case. In fact, in 1969, Pope Paul VI recanted that teaching, removing it from the General Roman Calendar to set the record straight. Regardless, Mary Magdalene still is seen by many in this light. This is such an important example of why we need to be so careful with our words and our study when we teach Scripture. The enemy will twist anything he can in order to deceive people about the goodness of God.

Another aspect of Mary that I love is the fact that she was a different kind of disciple than most of the rest. She followed Jesus because He was literally her Savior *before* He died. Jesus healed her and rescued her. Although the men were likely drawn in because of His love, she responded to His healing. If you missed it or weren't able to find it on your own, you can read about that in Luke 8.

Did you pick up the second important tidbit in Luke 8? You can find it in verse 3. What do you see there?

Luke points out how the women supported Jesus with their own resources. This helps us to understand that women not only had access to such resources, but used what they had to serve the Lord.

Another aspect about Mary you may have missed was shown to us in John 19:25. If you missed that, go ahead and look it up, making note of what we learn here.

Mary Magdalene was one of the women present at the cross. It is so interesting to me that almost none of the male disciples are mentioned in the final moments of Jesus' life. We don't find them placed at the scene of the crucifixion. We have no record of where they went. But we do know that Mary Magdalene was present. Do you remember what we learned earlier in this study about women being a witness? The testimony of women did not hold up in the Jewish court system. Yet, one of the key witnesses to the death of Jesus, and later the resurrection, was a woman. This is identified in all four gospels. There's some power there, Sis. Jesus values the testimony of women, regardless of what other, larger establishments value.

As we look at the final scene together, I hope it has become more and more clear to you that Jesus not only values women but chooses them to do Kingdom work.

We watch Mary come face to face with Jesus. Although her eyes do not recognize Him at first (vs 14), what does the Scripture say about her recognition of Him? (vs 16)

She recognized Jesus because of His voice. When He called her name.

When He calls her name, *she hears*.

Do you get it, Sis? The deepest longing of our hearts is to hear Jesus call our names, and I want that for you. I want you to recognize Him when He calls your name.

What happens next? What instruction does Jesus give to her? (vs 17)

The first person who the resurrected Christ reveals Himself to is a woman.

The first person Jesus sends to share the powerful message of the resurrection with others is a woman.

When we understand that, understand the responsibility we have as women to share Jesus with those around us, I believe we will respond in the same way Mary Magdalene does. We will *run* to those we are in relationship with and share the same message. What does Mary say when she reaches the disciples? (vs 18)

Her testimony is that first she heard the Lord, then she recognized Him and saw Him. I think it's the same for us. We study God's Word, and we hear Him speak, even if we can't see Him at first. Then, once we recognize His voice, we come to recognize not only where He is but what He has called us to do.

I have seen the Lord. Have you seen Him, Sis? Have you heard Him?

My earnest prayer is that the Lord would call a generation of women to rise up and declare this message—this message of hope, of the good news of the gospel, to a lost and hurting world.

My earnest prayer is that you would not keep this message to yourself, but that you would be the catalyst to a wave of healing and restoration in your home, your church, your city.

My earnest prayer is that you would use this study as the starting point that creates a hunger to know and learn the Word for yourself.

So that we as a generation of women can declare:

WHEN HE CALLS HER NAME,

she hears.